TELEVISION AND ETHNIC MINORITIES:
PRODUCERS' PERSPECTIVES

For Lucy

Television and Ethnic Minorities: Producers' Perspectives

A study of BBC In-house, Independent and Cable TV Producers

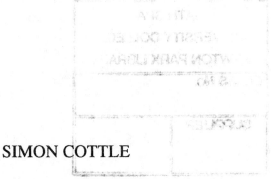

SIMON COTTLE

With a contribution by Patrick Ismond

Avebury

Aldershot • Brookfield USA • Hong Kong • Singapore • Sydney

Published by
Avebury
Ashgate Publishing Limited
Gower House
Croft Road
Aldershot
Hants GU11 3HR
England

Ashgate Publishing Company
Old Post Road
Brookfield
Vermont 05036
USA

British Library Cataloguing in Publication Data
Cottle, Simon, 1956-
    Television and ethnic minorities : producers' perspectives
    : a study of BBC In-house, Independent and Cable TV producers
    1.British Broadcasting Corporation 2.Ethnic television
    broadcasting - Great Britain 3.Television - Great Britain -
    Production and direction
    I.Title
    791.4'565'20693

Library of Congress Catalog Card Number: 96-79841

ISBN 1 85972 502 3

Printed in Great Britain by Ipswich Book Company, Suffolk

Contents

List of Tables

Acknowledgements

The research reported in these pages originally formed part of a wider research programme, 'Ethnic Minorities and Television', directed by Professor J.D. Halloran of the Centre for Mass Communication Research, University of Leicester. Professor Halloran kindly invited me to conduct a study of television producers and their experiences of, and perspectives on, the production of television programmes made by, for or about ethnic minorities. Like so many others working in the field of mass communications across the years, I owe Professor Halloran a debt of gratitude for this and other research opportunities granted and encouraged - many of which have also addressed important concerns of 'race', racism and minority ethnicity. Always supportive, but never unduly directive, Professor Halloran has proved to be a generous ally of research. Simply, the study would not have taken place without his original support.

The research principally took the form of a series of semi-structured interviews with a wide range of television producers currently involved in, or actively aspiring to be involved in, the production of minority ethnic television programmes. Interviews were thus conducted with both BBC in-house and independent producers, experienced and senior producers as well as those relatively new to the television production scene. My colleague Dr. Patrick Ismond helped carry out some of these interviews. Patrick has also contributed two chapters developed from his recent PhD research. Based on two case studies of cable television *narrowcasting* to ethnic minority audiences, his discussion provides critical insights and commentary on the representational practices of cable, as well as the ways in which this new communication technology is constrained and shaped within the marketplace. His contribution is very much appreciated and helps complement the rest of the study with its focus on *broadcasting* and the production of minority ethnic programmes. I would also like to thank Dr. Caroline New for her keen editing eye, Christine Eden and Bath College of Higher Education for their continuing support of research, Jan Skinner and Helen Duckett for transcribing most of the interviews, Christine Flenley for preparing the original research report, and Keith Davis for typesetting the re-written manuscript for book publication.

The study is indebted to all the above. The main debt of thanks must go, however, to those producers who generously offered their time, thoughts and considerable insights into the production of minority ethnic television. It is testimony to their commitment to the production of improved minority ethnic programming that they have volunteered accounts of, and commentary and criticism on, the institutional arrangements and practices of television production, notwithstanding their vulnerable institutional positions vis-à-vis corporate controllers, commissioners and other senior decision-makers and funders. It is for this reason that their anonymity has been protected throughout the study. In general organisational terms, however, I would like to thank the following for their participation: the BBC Multicultural Programmes Department (now Asian Programmes Department); independent collectives and production companies - Black Pyramid, Black Scorpio, Hall Place Studios, Indigo Productions, New Image, Non-Aligned Communications, Orchid Productions, Truth, Light, Action, and Wave Nation; and Cable TV operators AsiaVision/AsiaNet and Identity TV.

1 Introduction

This study aims to redress a lacuna in the research literature about television and ethnic minorities (1). Though countless studies have sought to examine television's representations of Britain's black and ethnic minorities in terms of the patterns, forms and discourses of media output, none has sought to go 'behind the scenes' and examine in detail, and from the practitioners' perspectives, the production of minority ethnic programmes (2). Programme makers as well as cultural critics, of course, have an important contribution to make to the wider debate about the 'proper' aims of minority ethnic programming; importantly, they alone can provide exclusive insights into the complexities, difficulties and dilemmas confronted by minority ethnic producers when making, or seeking to make, ethnic minority programmes. Without a full appreciation of the different institutional contexts and programme-making regimes shaping programme production across the television industry, as well as the diverse professional aims and cultural politics of representation enacted by different producers, critics are poorly placed to understand the parameters and constraints shaping those programmes later subjected to analysis and (often heated) debate. This is not to say, of course, that critical engagement with media output is not vitally necessary, simply that it remains insufficient if we want to understand better (and possibly intervene to realign) the forces currently shaping programme representations. This study, in modest terms, begins to redress this research imbalance.

This introductory chapter first elaborates on the argument above, contextualising the study's principal aim in relation to the wider field of mass communication research concerned with 'race', racism and ethnicity. This is then followed by a few words about its chosen methodology and the prominent role granted to producers' interview statements before, finally, an overview of the study's structure of presentation is outlined.

Mass communications research, 'race' and ethnicity: Theoretical context

There are few subjects more serious and deserving of detailed research than the role(s) played by the mass media in maintaining and reproducing racialised discourses, forms of racial inequality and boundaries of ethnic inclusion and exclusion (3). In a period when an increasingly 'Fortress' Europe has witnessed a resurgence of extreme racist violence and attempted genocide carried out under the chilling euphemism of 'ethnic cleansing', no one can doubt the importance of attending to the possible involvement of the mass media in such processes. To date, research in the UK has generally tended to examine the nature of mainstream media output at the level of black and ethnic minority *representations*, whether in relation to press and broadcast news, or television, film and other entertainment media and genres (4).

Numerous studies of news and 'race', for example, have generally arrived at similar conclusions. Across the years, and seemingly as a matter of routine, Britain's black and ethnic minorities have tended to be depicted in terms of a restricted repertoire of representations and/or within contexts characterised by conflict, controversy and deviance. In the 1960s and 1970s studies observed how immigrants were reported in relation to public health scares, problems of 'numbers' and tensions of 'race relations' - effectively concealing problems of British racism (Butterworth, 1967; Hartmann, Husband and Clarke,1974; Critcher et

2

al, 1977; Troyna, 1981). In the 1970s and across the 1980s studie identified the ways in which the moral panic orchestrated aroun 'mugging' and portrayal of street violence and inner city disorders served to criminalise Britain's black population - ignoring continuing social inequalities and growing anger at policing practices and harassment (Hall et al, 1978; Holland, 1981; Tumber, 1982; Murdock, 1984; Hansen and Murdock, 1985; Cottle, 1993a). In the 1980s and 1990s studies have charted the virulent press attacks on anti-racism campaigns, the vilification of black representatives and the seeming endorsement of statements of 'new racism' by prominent politicians - actively disparaging attempts to further multicultural and anti-racist agendas (Murray, 1986; Gordon and Rosenberg, 1989; Van Dijk, 1991). Widening the media lens to include film and television entertainment genres, Karen Ross, in her review of studies, has recently concluded: 'It is the poverty of black images rather than their frequency that constitutes the real problem, images constrained and constructed within a narrow band of character types in comedy and drama, or fetishized within a racialized demonology in factual programming. It is the lack of diversity when constructing black images as a well as the pejorative or negative connotations which such images provoke which lie at the centre of the representation debate in the media mainstream' (Ross, 1996, p. 170) - a finding echoing numerous other studies conducted across the years (Hartmann and Husband, 1974; Barry, 1988; Twitchin, 1988; Hall, 1990). General conclusions such as these, then, paint a depressing picture of the media's representations of ethnic minorities.

As *general* findings they can permit exceptions however. For example, a study of regional television news production and output has argued that differences in news form and programme ambitions occasionally allow for a more 'positive' and multiculturalist orientation to both its news subject matter and audience (Cottle, 1993b). A combination of factors has produced this differentiated news outcome, including: a developing newsroom awareness of multiculturalism; the pursuit of minority ethnic audiences as a means of increasing the programme rating; and the programme's populist 'visualisation', enacted daily by the producers, which informs the mix of selected news stories as well as their subject treatment. The historical development of TV programmes about and/or aimed at ethnic minority communities, also demonstrates important developments in the evolving relationship between television and ethnic minority audiences (Daniels and Gerson, 1989; Pines, 1992; Daniels, 1994; Ross, 1996). That history proves instructive for this study.

Following Daniels (1994), for example, and in broad strokes, the pictures of black people offered by television in the late 1940s to mid 1950s were confined to American entertainers, had an anthropological theme and/or were about the colonies. Following immigration in the 1950s and 1960s programmes responded to white anxieties about immigration and 'race relations' often by seeking to explain black ways of life to white audiences. It was not until the 1960s that programming for, in contrast to about, black people was produced though this was typically conceived as an educational service helping Asian immigrants to learn English and assimilate into British society. In the 1970s political struggles were waged for increased access to the television industry and improved representations outside of a narrow range of roles and negative treatments (Wadsworth, 1986; Tulloch, 1990). In this period competing positions on the politics of 'race' were played out through positions of 'multiculturalism' and 'anti-racism'. In the 1980s, with the advent of Channel Four, a burgeoning independent black workshop sector and continuing struggles for black representation both on and behind screen, the volume and range of programming aimed at black audiences began to increase. In the 1990s, however, some of the gains of the 1980s now look under threat as a shift away from public service ideals to the marketplace has restricted both funding and access, and apparently contributed to the development of 'sensationalist' and/or 'sexy' programmes at the expense of more serious forms of black programming. Culturally the late 1980s and 1990s have also witnessed increasing calls for a more differentiated understanding of minority ethnic communities and cultures, as the former politicised notion of 'black' begins to fragment under the new politics of identity, problematising calls for more accurate 'black' representation. This, admittedly crude, sketch of television's changing historical relation to and portrayal of black and

4

Asian minorities nonetheless indicates that television, as an institution and set of representational practices, has undergone a marked process of historical change and development, and will no doubt continue to do so. For our purposes it also suggests that a definite, intimate and recoverable relationship exists between the changing volume, range and nature of programmes produced for ethnic minority audiences on the one hand, and the changing institutional arrangements of broadcasting and surrounding cultural politics of 'race' on the other.

Interestingly, alongside the recent historical recovery of a more differentiated and historically developmental pattern of televisual representations of Britain's black and ethnic minority communities, has come a more sophisticated approach to the analysis of 'representations'. For example, the well-used notion of 'stereotype', often deployed in the analysis of media representations of 'race', has become problematised as the complexities of representations are opened up for more detailed textual discussion. This is not the place to engage with the details of such debates; suffice to say, however, that the concept 'stereotype', *inter alia,* is vulnerable to a number of criticisms (Mercer, 1989; Daniels, 1990; Cottle, 1992: 35-41; 1996). These include an evident confusion and slippage in the concept's status as a universal feature of processes of perception and cognition, and its more socially motivated and ideological roles. Competing realist and idealist premises have also informed the analysis of stereotypes and strategies of cultural engagement - should images represent, and possibly thereby legitimate, current racial(ised) distinctions and inequalities, or represent a more egalitarian and/or differentiated state of affairs, thereby largely ignoring the present while providing the cultural resources for change? The idea of 'stereotype' as an unproblematic and self-evident property found *in* the text also fails to consider the active work of historically/politically situated audiences in making stereotypes 'mean', or mean something different to that originally intended, or perhaps not mean at all - in other words, the *act* of audience interpretation proves crucial to the generation of meanings. The pursuit of 'stereotypes' has also tended to pulverise the textual complexity and coherence of representations which may in fact 'work' according to textual properties other than simple character portrayal. The role of narrative, audience expectations of different genres, and the increasing use of irony, for example, all problematise the easy assumption that representations, and their associated meanings, can best be captured with reference to stereotypes.

Studies which have managed, nonetheless, to rework something of the critical edge of the concept of stereotype into a more historically specific usage are the following (Hall, 1988; Wilson and Gutierrez, 1995, pp.150-167). Hall's discussion is of particular interest here and draws attention to the relevance of historical and political periodisation for any discussion of stereotypes and strategies of cultural engagement. In discussing black film-making in Britain, he observes first a historical moment of critique grounded in a common experience of marginalisation and racism in which 'black' becomes mobilised as a category of resistance and in which ethnic and cultural differences become subordinated to the politics of opposition. Importantly, he states: 'this analysis formulated itself in terms of a critique of the way blacks were positioned as the unspoken and invisible "other" of predominantly white aesthetic and cultural discourses.... There was a concern not simply with the absence or marginality of the black experience but with its simplification and its stereotypical character' (Hall, 1988, p.27). This moment, and its associated strategy of resistance, therefore sought to secure access to the rights of representation and contest the marginality and stereotypical images of blacks with a counter-position of 'positive' black images. Emerging from this historical moment, however, is a discerned new moment of black cultural engagement which recognises ethnic diversity and subjective identities and the ways in which each is crossed and re-crossed by 'race', ethnicity, gender, sexuality and diaspora histories, marking the end of 'the essential black subject'. Now the struggle over cultural representation is less about substituting 'positive' images for 'negative' ones, and more about engaging with the politics of difference and diversity, challenging ideas about stable or fixed ethnic identities - whether stereotypically represented as 'negative'

6

or 'positive'. Hall's observations are incisive and provide the means for a more sophisticated approach to the critical engagement with, and appreciation of, film and television's representations now approached in politically and historically proximate ways. To what extent producers of minority ethnic television programmes are also informed by a similar appreciation of the historically shifting cultural politics of representation, and seek to intervene within this, is clearly of considerable interest and is pursued across the study. Hall's penetrating insights nonetheless remain undeveloped in relation to an analysis of the institutional changes of film and television production.

Changing institutional arrangements and production regimes are also, of course, implicated in those emergent shifts in the cultural politics of representation. A recent examination of American television, which maps the evolving nature of programme representations in relation to the surrounding politics of 'race' and changing institutional arrangements of television, proves instructive in this respect (Gray, 1995). Little work to date, however, has been directed at the regulatory policy frameworks and commercial forces informing British broadcasting and their impact upon the production of minority ethnic programme making. Exceptions include a discussion of market forces and the marginalization of black film and video production (Hussein, 1994) and doctoral research on British media policies and minority media production (Ismond, 1994). More general discussions of British broadcasting and recent processes of change, generally analysed as a move away from public service broadcasting, also provide useful background discussion (Hood, 1994), especially those focusing on the British Broadcasting Corporation (BBC) and Independent Television companies (ITV) (Winston, 1994; Corner et al, 1994), Channel Four (Harvey, 1994), cable and telecommunications (Murdock, 1994) and the independent production sector (Robins and Cornford, 1992; Sparks, 1994).

Four winds of change can be acknowledged at the outset as providing important shaping forces to the production of ethnic minority television. These are, respectively, the changing regulatory context of broadcasting in the 1990s and institutional responses to this by the major television broadcasters and 'publishers' - the BBC, ITV companies and Channel Four; the development of 'new' technologies, satellite and cable particularly (5); intensified commercial imperatives and their effects upon programme commissioning, programme production and programme forms; and the changing cultural politics of 'race' and multiculturalism. Such broad contextualisation of minority ethnic programme production and portrayal provides a necessary backdrop to the more detailed commentary and discussion found in this study, and also provides a necessary complement to the developed cultural-political criticism of television's representations.

Institutionally positioned in between, and buffeted by, the forces of economic, regulatory and technological change on the one side, and the shifting sands of ethnic identity-politics and cultural political criticism of television's representations on the other, stand the television producers. By force of circumstance, then, producers have much to contribute to our understanding of the turbulent winds currently blowing and shaping minority ethnic programmes and they offer a vantage point from which to glimpse the immediate future. So far their professional practices and production contexts have received little serious inquiry, the inference being perhaps that these are relatively unimportant when set alongside the surrounding forces of the marketplace, government policy and new technologies. While these 'forces' exert, of course, a profound impact upon the production of ethnic minority programmes, they do not simply impose themselves but are actively negotiated and managed through institutional, organisational and professional means. People, in other words, are very much actively involved in such processes, professionally mediating the complex of forces that currently surround television and its programme production. Moreover, studies of media professionals (as discussed below) have typically revealed that other important factors are also at work, features too often lost from view when theoretical sights remain fixed upon the wider determinations of the marketplace, political regulation or new technologies.

Though little has been published about the production of minority ethnic television programmes, an area of related research interest concerns the black independent film and video sector of the 1980s and the work of a number of high-profile collectives and workshops including *Sankofa Film and Video*, *Black Audio Film Collective* and *Ceddo Film and Video*. This vibrant black cultural development, subsidised for a short period by Channel Four and, amongst others, the British Film Institute, produced politically engaged and, often, experimental and innovative films. The history of this moment in black film production has been described elsewhere (Pines, 1988; Hussein 1994; Ross, 1996), and the academic and theoretical reflection it unleashed on the possibly distinctive aesthetics and politics of black film continues (Hall, 1988; Mercer, 1988, 1994; Snead, 1994). In the 1990s the erosion of public subsidies and grants, changing television funding arrangements and general logic of the marketplace all appear to have contributed to the demise of this former moment of black creativity (Marsh-Edwards cited in Keighron and Walker, 1994), at the same time as the cultural politics of 'race' and ethnicity have also undergone change.

This study is not directly concerned with high-profile film and video collectives, however, but is more concerned with, amongst other sectors of television production, those independent organisations now working in close proximity to the television industry either as established independents producing programmes for the major television outlets or those who are actively seeking to do so. Hard and fast distinctions are difficult in this fluid area of productive activity. As we will see, the distinction between workshops or collectives and commercial production companies is now much less clear than in the 1980s; changing times have required different organisational responses (Robins and Cornford, 1992; Sparks, 1994).

As stated already, the study does not propose to research the current range and forms of minority ethnic programming via a comprehensive review and discussion of current programming (see Givanni, 1995; Ross, 1996), but it is perhaps useful at the outset to indicate something of the current state of play in contemporary minority ethnic programming. Stuart Hall, a leading academic in the field of the sociology and cultural politics of 'race', provides what I suspect many would consider a reasonable and fair appraisal of some of the gains and continu-

9

ing deficiencies of current television in this respect.

> Let us establish some of the broader parameters of the debate. Things have moved very rapidly in the 1980s and early 1990s. There is no denying the much greater visibility, the wider access, of black practitioners, black representations and black culture on British television.... Of course, these 'gains' have been extremely limited: limited in scale, limited in terms of key positions which blacks occupy in shaping long-term policy in the institution, and limited in the range and repertoire of black representations. That repertoire has a distinctive, peculiar lopsided, uneven and (in disconcerting ways) predictable shape: blacks everywhere on the screen transferred through sport; blacks increasingly in light entertainment, in TV popular culture and 'youth TV'; more black newscasters and presenters; some strategic breakthroughs in comedy; much more fitful and marginal in serious documentary and current affairs; and especially in arts features, serious drama, film and fiction. No one should read the acknowledgement that there have been gains as saying everything is rosy for black British programming in the television garden. Nevertheless, the baseline for the discussion must be that, at the same time as these limits are openly and explicitly registered and acknowledged, the fact of a shift in the growing black presence across the face of British television cannot be denied. (Hall, 1995, p. 14)

This study, with the help of producers of minority ethnic programmes, attends to the television garden of black and Asian programming in the middle to late 1990s. It digs into the normally invisible sub-soil of television production and examines the present state of cultivation. The principal concern is with the current situation as witnessed,

perceived, experienced, managed and negotiated by producers working both inside and outside the major television institutions. Too few
'insider' accounts of minority ethnic programme production have been
forthcoming and those there are have been confined to three, of only
four, senior positions occupied by black people in recent British
broadcasting (Phillips, 1992, 1995, 1996; Shah, 1992; Dhondy, 1992).
The study makes occasional reference to public statements by these,
and other, senior executives and commissioning editors, but its focus
remains on the accounts and perspectives offered by the programme
producers themselves.

Considerations of method and aims

Given the central role afforded to producers' comments and insights
secured through interviews, a few words on the research status granted
to these is in order. Speaking methodologically, the central role
granted to producers' comments should not be taken as indicating that
producers are assumed to have an omniscient view of all things
television, nor that they enjoy unfettered creative autonomy. Programme producers provide a key vantage point from which to better
view the operations of programme commissioning and production; as
such they help complement the critical findings secured by engaging
with programme output and/or those wider forces of the marketplace,
government regulation and new technologies. From their professional
understanding and experience of programme production, television
producers help provide information and insight into the complex of
forces, constraints *and* representational aims that variously inform
their professional practices as programme makers. Of course their
accounts do not simply describe the situation, but also tell us about
how such forces and settings are perceived, experienced, negotiated
and managed. In this sense, producer statements and accounts provide
a resource for understanding, a resource that has yet to be analysed and
integrated into a more comprehensive understanding of minority ethnic programme production. Furthermore, in so far as producers'
accounts demonstrate certain commitments, the pursuit and enactment

11

of professional norms, say, or particular positions on the cultural politics of representation, so their statements provide the basis for critical discussion as well as improved understanding. It would surely be a mistake to assume producers have unlimited professional autonomy or creative independence. Listening to the producers' accounts below, ideas of 'professional autonomy' and 'creative independence' for the most part appear to evaporate in the constrained and pressurised world of television production. In this respect, a recent study of television producers has provided by far a too 'rosy' picture of discerned professional autonomy (Tunstall, 1993), and has been critiqued elsewhere (Cottle, 1995a). Interestingly, this same study declined to investigate the extent of, or conditions confronted by, specifically minority ethnic producers - a major oversight in any study proclaiming a generalised situation of television producer well-being.

At this point it is useful to briefly refer to sociological studies of news journalism and production - by far the most developed area of research into media professionals and media production. These studies collectively point to the fallacy of singling out journalists and their attitudes as a sufficient means of understanding the nature, routines and forms of journalism (for reviews see: Cottle 1993c, 1997; Schudson, 1991). In the context of 'race' reporting, for example, the studies indicate that the explanation for racist reporting is a good deal more complicated than simply assuming that such can be accounted for with reference to the personal viewpoints and prejudices of individual journalists, senior editors or proprietors (Halloran, 1974; Cottle, 1994a). Research suggests, rather, that we need to situate the professional practices of journalists in relation to such wider influences and shaping contexts as: professional recruitment, training and socialisation; daily organisational routines and source dependencies; institutional hierarchy, policies and corporate ethos; market forces and competitive rivalries; 'news values', prevailing cultural discourses and embedded conventions of genre and form (Cottle, 1994a, 1994b, 1995b). In other words, the research on news journalism highlights the error of placing an explanatory burden upon the shoulders of the journalists themselves. Complex institutional arrangements and economic processes, themselves often shaped by and shaping of sur-

12

rounding social, cultural and political forces, rarely grant individuals an entirely free hand - even if the professional ideology of journalism suggests otherwise. That said, journalists have proved to be an invaluable source of insight into the professional ideology and practices of news journalism; and the more critical of them are also aware of the effects of the impinging contexts mentioned.

If the production of news is 'overdetermined' by a confluence of such forces, broadcasting generally and genre specifically is also, of course, subject to wider pressures and influences. Producers of minority ethnic programmes, as we shall hear, already feel they carry upon their shoulders a heavy 'burden of representation'. This study does not propose, then, to add to this weight with a simplistic pursuit of professional, much less, personal responsibility (or culpability) for programming assumed to be solely accountable in individualist terms. Programme makers, and would-be programme makers, currently stand in the 'eye of the storm', surrounded and buffeted by winds of change - regulatory, commercial, and cultural/political. They are ideally positioned - though few I suspect experience their position comfortably - to view and pronounce upon the difficulties and changing fortunes of producing minority ethnic programmes for British broadcasting *and* narrowcasting. In so far as producers steer a course through such stormy times and manage to reach their preferred programme destination they themselves, of course, also constitute a contributing force. Here it is permissible to comment upon and perhaps critically engage with the producers' views in so far as these inform the production of their programmes. Ideas enacted relating, say, to the changing and contested positions on 'multiculturalism' and the cultural politics of representation have undoubtedly, to some degree, informed organisational aims, programme visualisation, production and output across the years.

This study focuses deliberately upon three representative groups of producers of minority ethnic programming currently working in different sectors of the television industry. The research attends to BBC in-house producers, commercial and community-based independents, and, incorporating recent research by Patrick Ismond, cable TV operators. In broad terms it sets out to document and consider their respec-

13

tive aims, experiences and perspectives relating to the production of minority ethnic programmes. A further aim is to marshall these accounts into a thematically organised discussion in which constructive comment and criticism can be developed. The study necessariiy, therefore, draws extensively upon the testimonies of a wide range of television producers and practitioners. Their voices are deliberately given prominent and often lengthy exposure throughout the study. Of course, their voices, their accounts have been subject to the overall narrative framing this report. Statements have been selected, excerpted and ordered into chapter discussions, and these have been arranged for thematic and analytical convenience. Furthermore, interviews were conducted with the help of a semi-structured, open-ended interview schedule, loose and flexible but semi-structured nonetheless in relation to a number of broad areas of 'relevance'. Such is the inescapable responsibility of the researcher/author. Research is always informed by preceding theoretical ideas and numerous contexts, including those of its execution and delivery. As far as possible, however, the study aims to report faithfully the producers' own perspectives as revealed by the interviewees themselves in interviews designed to encourage open-ended discussion. It is the producers' accounts, *their* experiences and emphases, *their* arguments and viewpoints that form the 'stuff' of the report. These are subject to ordering, discussion and occasional critical comment but they remain a focal point of interest throughout.

Specifically the study asks: what have been the producers' experiences of producing minority ethnic programming within and for major broadcasting and narrowcasting television outlets? How do *they* define 'minority ethnic programming' and what do *they* see as its fundamental raison d'être; and how, if at all, have both evolved in recent years? What are the perceived difficulties and dilemmas of *their* situation vis-à-vis television institutions, television gatekeepers, television forms and television audiences? In what ways are representational practices informed by the changing cultural politics of 'race' and multiculturalism? How have the changing regulatory and institutional structures of broadcasting and new technologies impacted upon professional practices and wider opportunities for gaining entry to the television industry? From the vantage point of the middle to late 1990s what are *their* considered views on the future of minority ethnic programmes at local, regional, national and global levels?

The research is based on interviews with twenty television producers and makers of minority ethnic programmes, many of whom have experience of working in more than one of the sectors addressed - the BBC and its Multicultural Programme Department, the independent production sector, and cable TV. Seven people interviewed worked for the former BBC Multicultural Programmes Department (now Asian Programmes Department) at Pebble Mill studios in Birmingham. Those interviewed included an Executive Producer, Producer/Director, Producer, Assistant Producer, two Programme Researchers and a Trainee Researcher working across a range of African-Caribbean and Asian programmes, including documentaries, current affairs, magazine programmes and light entertainment. Ten independent producers were interviewed, six based in London, three in Bristol and one in Leeds. Some had previously worked for major television outlets including the BBC, are established independent producers and have a considerable track record of in-house and independent commissions. Others are relatively new and, hopefully, emergent producers in the field of television production who are seeking their first commissions. All had had dealings with Channel Four either seeking guidance and support, or commissions. The Executive Producer working at the BBC Multicultural Programmes Department had also worked previously at Channel Four and three of the independents had previously worked for the BBC. Most of the independents had also had dealings with the BBC and/or major regional ITV companies. Between them, therefore, this group of producers has considerable experience of in-house and independent production for the BBC, the pursuit of commissions for Channel Four and dealings with ITV companies. The study also draws upon interviews with three senior decision-makers working for the cable TV companies AsiaVision, succeeded by AsiaNet, and Identity TV. These professionals also had extensive experience of working for other sectors of the television industry including the BBC.

All interviews were taped and subsequently transcribed. They were semi-structured in form, with interviewees encouraged to identify and elaborate upon experiences, issues and concerns deemed important by them (see Appendix A for in-house and independent producer interview schedules). Basic factual information concerning personal biography and programme involvement was elicited, as were their ideas about their respective organisations' aims and general politics concerning minority ethnic television access, programme representation and producer accountability. Interviewees were asked about, and sometimes prompted to elaborate upon, their dealings with Channel Four and other potential commissioning television institutions. Basically, the interviews were open-ended and every attempt was made to encourage interviewees to identify, elaborate upon and emphasise those issues, experiences and concerns that they felt were the most pressing as far as they and their organisation were concerned. Most interviewees were happy to be tape-recorded and spoke at length about their experiences and concerns. All were given the opportunity for anonymity. Surprisingly, perhaps, none of the independent producers appeared concerned about anonymity, though it was stated by the interviewers at the outset that individuals would not be named in the published report. The BBC producers, in contrast, tended to be a little more wary about the research and more cautious about possible personal 'comeback'. Having said that, the author was struck by the candid nature of some of their comments and criticisms of the BBC. Again, it was promised to all concerned that their comments, in so far as it is possible, given their programme responsibilities, would remain anonymous. It can only be hoped that all who read the study take the producers' comments in the spirit that they were volunteered, that is, as considered and constructive contributions to wider public debate and understanding. It would be a disservice to their undoubted commitment to minority ethnic programming to seek to identify anybody involved in the research with a view to taking up with them personally the issues raised. It *is* hoped that the study may contribute to wider public debate and understanding however.

Structure of presentation

The study is structured in four parts. Part One looks at the aims, experiences, problems and perspectives of in-house producers working for the former Multicultural Programmes Department (now Asian Programmes Department) at the BBC. These producers work inside the traditional heartland of British public service broadcasting, daily pursuing programme goals and confronting institutionalised difficulties and obstacles. Their accounts offer a rare (unique even) set of insights into the professional programme makers environment as experienced from inside the BBC. The chapters, as with those in Part Two and Part Three, are organised thematically and deal respectively with: organisational/departmental aims; the cultural politics of representation; major controls, constraints and limitations; gatekeepers, commissioners and so-called 'sweethearts'; and, finally, views on ethnic minority programme production in the foreseeable future.

Part Two attends, in similar terms, to independent producers seeking programme commissions from major broadcasters. These producers, some working as established and successful commercial independents, others as 'emergent' and community-based programme makers, are on the outside of the major television institutions, seeking commissions from those on the inside. This critical relationship of dependence is explored at some length, as are the other themes and concerns noted above.

Part Three, written by Patrick Ismond, provides two case study discussions of minority ethnic cable television services, AsiaVision/AsianNet and Identity TV. Complementing the study of BBC and independent producers, his study examines how cable TV professionals currently 'circle the perimeter fence' of traditional terrestrial television broadcasting. Cable TV, with its possibilities for narrowcasting to minority ethnic audiences, promises enhanced representation and programme involvement and yet it is also subject to the most acute pressures of commercialism and the marketplace. How this struggle has been played out and informed the operations of two different cable TV services, one aimed at Asian, the other at African-Caribbean audiences, forms the basis of this third part of the study. The two case study discussions also address questions of professional aims, informing cultural politics of representation, and various structural constraints and limitations experienced by the cable operators, and a conclusion relating to both is provided at the end of Part Three.

Part Four, finally, pulls some of the threads together in conclusion and provides a number of critical observations on the state of television and minority ethnic programme production, as well as identifying necessary lines for future research. Each of the three substantive discussions, dealing with, respectively, BBC in-house producers, independents, and cable TV operators, can be read as separate, self-contained studies. Read together, however, they provide a more comprehensive overview of, and critical insight into, the current state of British broadcasting and narrowcasting in relation to the production of minority ethnic programming. As such they help provide improved understanding of a fast-changing television landscape and the ways in which this continues to shape and limit the range and forms of television programmes, both mainstream and special provision, concerned with ethnic minorities. If the study helps to contribute to a wider understanding of the differentiated professional aims, difficulties and dilemmas now influencing (and constraining) the production of ethnic minority programmes across the current TV landscape, its principal aim will have been met.

Notes

1 The politics of 'race' and ethnicity informs the politics of language use and language choices. A note on the use of language in this report is therefore necessary. Historically the language and semantics of 'race' have undergone processes of contestation and change. While the term 'black' came to signify a politically encompassing reference to marginalised minority groups in the UK in the 1970s and 1980s, the term 'black' increasingly refers to specifically British African-Caribbean people in the 1990s in recognition of important differences between African-Caribbean and Asian groups. 'African-

Caribbean' and 'Asian' groups can also, of course, be referenced with further precision, in terms of place of family origin, language, religion and generation as context demands. The term 'ethnic minority' currently is widely used, and is used throughout this study. It too can be contested however. Unfortunately some people have used it as a substitution or code word for 'race', just as the word 'immigrant' was used in the recent past. When used this way, the speaker proclaims him/herself to have moved beyond a spurious biological categorisation of people into 'races', while nonetheless either maintaining such a covert belief or continuing to harbour ideas of social distinction, even superiority and inferiority, now referenced through deep-seated traditions and 'cultural' differences. The term 'ethnic minority' can also imply perhaps that 'ethnicity' is a defining characteristic of minority, not majority, groups. Some people thus prefer the term 'minority ethnics' or 'minority ethnic groups'. Approached from a different cultural-political stance others may find the positive privileging of the internal 'cultural' signified by the term 'ethnicity' insufficiently inflected in relation to the external politics of exclusion that has informed recent mobilisations of the term 'black'. Language choices, then, are profoundly political and essentially contested; historically terms often become challenged and replaced, or semantically 'reoriented' to accommodate new sets of signified meanings.

This study generally uses the terms 'ethnic minorities' and 'ethnic minority television programmes' when addressing concerns of special programme provision, and uses more specific terms as the context of discussion demands. Given the identified problems with the term, a defence of its continuing use is perhaps necessary. The term 'ethnic minorities' continues to be widely used as a descriptive shorthand and provides therefore useful common ground; it is also of particular relevance and use in relation to the study's object of analysis (the production of special provision television programming). It is not necessarily implicated as a 'code' word for 'race', and neither does it necessarily imply a delimited view of ethnicity as confined to minority, in contrast to dominant, social groups. It continues, in other words, to have common acceptance and descriptive value. In the context of this study, the use of the term 'ethnic minorities' should not be assumed, however, to imply an acceptance of a particular multiculturalist agenda, and certainly does not imply an endorsement of a position of 'ethnic absolutism' or primordialism. As is often the case, context helps determine the ideological and other uses of key terms. Sometimes 'African-Caribbean' or 'black' and 'Asian' will also be used or further refined with reference, for example, to 'Asian Muslims' or the 'Bangladeshi community', again as appropriate to the context of discussion. Recent commentary on the cultural politics and complexity of black identity with reference to the end of 'the essential black subject', as discussed later in this chapter, points once again to the historically changing and politically fluid nature of identity and alerts us all to the potential tyranny of imposed categories.

2   Three partial exceptions to this bold claim can be noted. An early research report 'Television in a Multi-Racial Society' (Anwar and Shang, 1982), as well as monitoring ethnic minority appearances across television's output, also included summary data drawn from a questionnaire administered to programme controllers, producers and directors. Though suggested at the time, the study was not followed up with a more in-depth exploration of 'attitudes', its chosen focus of inquiry. An early, and in many respects innovative, study of the making of a television documentary series 'The Nature of Prejudice' provides insightful discussion of production processes (Elliott, 1972) and deserves to be repeated with similar attention to detail. A more recent study of local radio and ethnic minorities also confirms the value of attending to production considerations and draws upon producers' interview statements to elicit an informing 'integrationist ethos', concern with 'balance', and also notes the effects of poor resources on 'meaningful speech' (Husband and Chouhan, 1985). For my part, my recent study of regional television news production and representations of

'race' (Cottle 1993a, 1993b, 1994b) has sought to attend to the complex of production forces shaping news representations, and my study of Central Television (Cottle, 1993a) also included some discussion of the production environment, producer goals and 'programme visualisation' informing an ethnic minority magazine programme (Cottle, 1993a, pp. 201-10).

Both minority audiences and minority media have, until recently, also received relatively little research interest by mass communication researchers. This study contributes to discussion of television in relation to the latter (for an insightful discussion of the British Punjabi press and surrounding constraints, see Tatla and Singh, 1989). For studies which have sought to engage with questions of minority audience use of, and response to, minority media see (Jones and Dungey, 1983; Halloran, Bhatt and Gray, 1995; Gillespie, 1995).

3 This study is principally interested in the production of television programmes aimed at ethnic minority groups and communities. It examines the production of programmes made by, for and/or about ethnic minorities. These programmes generally aim to represent or given expression to collective minority identities, interests and concerns and can act as a resource for a more *positive* endorsement and mobilisation of ethnic minority identities and cultures in contrast to the often restrictive and *negative* repertoire of mainstream portrayals of 'race' implicated in processes of racism and racialisation. The view of 'ethnic minority' informing this study is broadly a sociological one where the members of such a group 'are usually thought not only to share a measure of common culture often exhibited by religion and language, but also to participate together in social institutions, to have a certain shared social organisation and purposeful 'membership' which the members, in some sense, assert' (Fenton, 1996, p.144). Such an approach has the virtue of highlighting social relations and organisation as well as a sense of collective purpose, whether originated from within the group or perhaps in response to external conditions. Minority ethnicity, in other words, is not a narrowly conceived 'cultural affair' perhaps

21

approached in the manner of individuals shopping around for a cultural overcoat; rather, it is a dynamic, often internally contested and externally informed response in which tradition and custom, not to mention language, religion and historical narratives, provide the collective means of making sense of, and engaging with, the conditions of the present. When approached in such terms ethnic minority television programmes can, potentially at least, provide resources helping to sustain, express and assert ethnic minority identities, cultures and interests, contributing arguments, ideas and symbols of possible use in processes of identity formation and change.

This informing view of minority ethnicity as a dynamic, collective and often contested process is not at work in the latest 1991 British Census however. Here findings about 'ethnic minorities' are based upon an amalgam of individual responses, each seemingly self-selected from a pre-defined list of 'ethnic identities', which together provide a relatively static, albeit administratively convenient, overview of Britain's ethnic minority populations (Fenton, 1996). With this proviso in mind the 1991 Census, summarised by one of the authors of an official study, calculates: 'Britain's ethnic minorities number just over 3 million out of a population of 55 million - 5.5 percent. South Asians make up nearly half this total. Indians numbered 840,000, Pakistanis 477,000, Bangladeshis 163,000. The Chinese numbered 157,000. The Caribbean population numbered 500,000, the Africans 212,000' (Peach, 1996, p.17). Important inter and intra-minority differences of socio-economic circumstances characterise all these groups including employment and training, housing, educational attainment and life-chances (Jones, 1993; Peach, 1996), deep-seated factors that should not be forgotten in the current academic enthusiasm directed at 'cultural' processes of identity formation and difference (for a useful review of current theoretical positions on 'race', racism and new ethnicities, see Solomos and Back, 1996).

4 What follows is a brief review only of the research literature and findings. The voluminous mass communications research on

'race', racism and ethnicity has been reviewed in more detailed discussion in the following (Cottle, 1992; Ross, 1996).

5 As Murdock charts in his discussion, cable television is, in fact, not that 'new', with the first cable systems built in the 1920s to relay regular broadcast services to areas with poor reception (Murdock, 1994). Importantly, his discussion also charts the ways in which this particular communication technology, both before and after the innovation of fibre-optics and increased carrying capacity, has been driven by, and regulated in relation to, market considerations.

With regard to cable and satellite's involvement in ethnic minority television the Independent Television Commission (ITC) describes a number of services that currently operate under its licences. These include satellite services: *TV Asia, Middle East Broadcasting, Japan Satellite TV, China News Europe* and *Muslim Television Ahmadiyya*. Services available to cable viewers include *AsiaVision* (now *AsiaNet* discussed in Part Three) launched in 1986 which broadcasts programmes in Hindi, Urdu, Punjabi, Bengali, Gujrati and Tamil, mainly acquired from the Indian sub-continent; *Identity Television,* launched in 1993, is aimed primarily at African-Caribbeans and is the UK's only dedicated black entertainment channel; *Namaste*, started in 1992, is owned by the Gandhi Corporation and aimed at the Asian community, providing programming including drama, movies, documentaries and general entertainment mostly acquired from independent distributors in the UK (ITC, 1994).

Part One
On the Inside Looking Out:
BBC Producers

I just feel sometimes that we cop out and that we water down, we are just not aggressive, perhaps that's the wrong word, but we're just not progressive in exploring the issues facing our community purely because we are scared of the backlash we would face. Because there's not many Asian programmes on TV our department is the focus and it has the most physical profile, so we have to be very careful. So I can undersatnd the attitude. And, also, you know, we work for the BBC as well. We have to be very careful. (BBC Producer)

2 Aims, access and accountability

The BBC and ethnic minorities: The public face

Britain's public service broadcaster, the BBC, proclaims itself to be fully committed to the task of enhancing ethnic minority representation:

> The BBC has a particular duty to represent and serve Britain's ethnic minorities. This is not just because we have a responsibility to meet the needs of *all* our licence payers, but because the BBC is one of the key institutions through which all of us form a picture of the kind of society Britain is: whether it is inclusive or exclusive; whether it recognises and celebrates the value of cultural and ethnic diversity or falls back on old stereotypes and prejudice; whether it strives to increase mutual understanding and equality of opportunity or is content to allow hostility and disadvantage to persist.
>
> For many years, the BBC has a particular duty to represent and serve its ethnic minority audiences properly, both through targeted programmes and

services and through fair representation in mainstream radio and television output. (BBC, 1995, *People and Programmes*, p.163)

Since 1983 the Corporation has had an agreed equal opportunities policy, and the stated aim throughout the BBC is to reflect the ethnic composition of the nation in both its programmes and its workforce. To this end the employment policy of the BBC aims to 'eradicate discrimination and find ways of dealing with it wherever it arises'; 'select, promote and treat staff solely on the basis of their relevant qualifications and abilities'; 'actively encourage staff ... to take advantage of the BBC's equal opportunities policy and, where appropriate training opportunities'; and 'monitor gender, ethnic composition and disability of the workforce and job applicants and to set and meet targets over a period' (BBC, 1993, *Producer Choice*). In addition, the selection of suppliers and contracts for buying resources include Equal Opportunity clauses, encouraging good practice in the television industry and related fields more widely. Clearly the BBC has publicly committed itself to equal opportunities in relation to its workforce and enhanced representation at the level of special and mainstream programmes. Programmes are transmitted in the public domain and are, of course, available to be seen.

The Corporation has proved less transparent, however, when it comes to making data available about the ethnic composition of its workforce - data clearly necessary if we are to determine the success or otherwise of its Equal Opportunities policy and initiatives to increase ethnic minority recruitment. (My personal experience of dealing with the BBC in this respect can only be likened, proverbially, to 'getting blood out of a stone' - an experience recounted by others researching in the field.) The limited data made publicly available is highly selective and often hopelessly blunt. The 1994/95 *Report and Accounts*, for example, includes one table entitled 'Equal opportunities initiatives' (BBC, 1995b, p.97) which summarises the proportion of ethnic minorities in London Based Directorates and Regions. The picture presented appears highly promising in the London directorates (though not the regions), with the 8 percent target for the year 2000 already exceeded in many directorates. Unfortunately no information is presented concerning the actual posts occupied by ethnic minority personnel or where these fall within the corporate hierarchy (a key omission). Also unhelpful is the failure to indicate which social groups are included under the title 'ethnic minority'. Given the BBC's declaration that 'our most pressing concern is for Britain's largest and most visible ethnic minorities - the Asian and African-Caribbean communities' (BBC, 1995a, p.164), this is a surprising and potentially misleading omission. The term 'ethnic minority' can of course prove to be highly elastic, capturing all kinds of culturally differentiated groups, many of whom may not have experienced the same historical, and contemporary, conditions of discrimination and disadvantage - fundamental differences any Equal Opportunities employer must recognise and act upon. Following repeated requests for more detailed information about ethnic minority involvement within the BBC's workforce, the BBC's Equal Opportunity Advisor told the author that this information was not known to her and could only be gained from the Head, Corporate Human Resource Planning - a curious position for any 'Equal Opportunities Advisor' to find themselves in. The Head, Corporate Human Resource Planning, informed me that the BBC 'cannot differentiate between "mainstream" and "special provision" TV programming in relation to our ethnic monitoring procedures. Data on employees is collected at Directorate level (e.g. Network Television, Network Radio, Regional Broadcasting) and is not programme specific. Staff tend to move frequently between programmes, making it impossible to pin down monitoring data at this level.' Repeated requests for general data, however, concerning ethnic minority involvement throughout the BBC and in relation to corporate hierarchies were ignored.

Some data was finally provided though this remains blunt and undifferentiated in terms of different ethnic minority groups. Within Network Television as a whole 6.4 percent of staff said to be involved in production (that is, excluding those involved in finance, secretarial, administrative roles) are recorded as 'African', 'Asian', 'Caribbean' or 'black other'. To what extent these different groups are represented across different production occupational groups remains undisclosed.

Ethnic minority groups (as defined above) are said to comprise 4 percent of the BBC producer population. Eight percent of associate producers belong to ethnic minorities and among assistant producers and script editors - distinct jobs but both feeder routes to full producer status - 11 percent are from ethnic minorities. These variations are clearly associated with length of service in the BBC. As the Head, Corporate Human Resource Planning, explained: 'Ethnic minority staff are, on average, more recent recruits than their white European colleagues and have not yet gained sufficient experience to be fully represented at producer level. However, the evidence shows that the picture is changing and that ethnic minority staff are moving ahead rapidly.' Table 2.1, provided by the BBC, indicates this reported change.

Table 2.1
Ethnic minorities and BBC programme production

Occupational group	% from ethnic minorities	Average length of BBC service: ethnic minorities	Average length of BBC service: white European
Assistant Producer/ Script Editor	11%	2.7 years	5.6 years
Assistant Producer	8%	4.3 years	11.2 years
Producer	4%	6 years	9.7 years

As indicated above, the deficit of available information concerning ethnic minority involvement by different ethnic minority groups, and in relation to both production and non-production occupations throughout the BBC, provides an impoverished basis for appraising the Corporation's public claims and statements of intent. Whether the lack of data reflects poor monitoring or simply Corporate reluctance to publicly share such information, the fact remains that the BBC's public statements of commitment to equal opportunities and ethnic minorities are likely to ring hollow if such information remains unavailable. Accurate and detailed monitoring, of course, forms a necessary part of any Equal Opportunities programme seriously committed to activating change. Given the public service remit of the BBC and its dependence upon the public's licence fee, strong grounds exist of course for arguing that the Corporation has a responsibility to make such information publicly available. While Table 2.1 certainly appears to indicate that ethnic minorities are making significant headway in relation to production occupations, as stated, this should be contextualised in relation to the BBC workforce as a whole and further specified with reference to particular ethnic minority groups.

This study's principal aim, however, is to look behind the BBC's public statements of intent and available statistics and examine, from the producers' point of view, their experiences and possible difficulties encountered when making ethnic minority programmes. Interestingly, the BBC has publicly declared itself to be fully supportive of its producers:

> The BBC's success depends on its relationship with two key groups of people: those who watch and listen to our programmes - the audience; and those who make our programmes - the creative talent.
> Without a strong bond of understanding with our audience, we run the risks of self-indulgence, elitism and, in the new age of broadcasting choice, irrelevance.
> Without a strong bond with our talent, we will find it impossible to meet the standards of quality and originality which our audience rightly demands. (BBC, 1995a, *People and Programmes*, p.1)

And, with specific reference to ethnic minorities, the BBC has unequivocally stated:

> - we must ensure we successfully reach reasonable numbers of all the main minority groups with programmes specifically targeted at them, whether on radio or television, national or local,

31

- we must ensure that there is adequate and fair representation of ethnic minorities in all mainstream programmes of all kinds,

- we must work still harder to recruit and develop Black African-Caribbean and Asian programme makers. (BBC, 1995a, *People and Programmes*, p.168)

The remainder of Part One now turns to examine these commitments, from the inside as it were, and consults a number of BBC in-house producers who are involved in the production of special provision or 'targeted' ethnic minority programmes. The study now focuses, therefore, on producers working within the Multicultural Programmes Department, the BBC's department with special responsibilities for making ethnic minority programmes.

The BBC Multicultural Programmes Department: Background and aims

In September 1991 the BBC Multicultural Programmes Department was created, bringing together the previously separate Asian and African-Caribbean Units at the BBC Pebble Mill Centre in Birmingham. Four years later, in September 1995, it was announced that the Multicultural Programmes Department was now to be disbanded. An Asian Programmes Department would continue to produce and commission programmes at Pebble Mill, while an Executive Producer was to be appointed to oversee the commissioning of programmes for the African-Caribbean audience from Manchester. Unlike Asian programmes, these are now no longer produced by a dedicated team of producers but are commissioned from independents and in-house producers working in the various mainstream BBC departments of Drama, Entertainment, Youth and Entertainment Features, Music and Arts, and Education for Adults. As the former Managing Editor of the Multicultural Programmes Department, Narendhra Morar, has stated: 'This area of programme-making has had a long, chequered and

32

sometimes, controversial history' (Morar, 1995: 2). This most recent development has proved to be no less controversial, and once again raises questions about the aims, representational strategies and appropriate role of special programming provision for minority ethnic communities produced within the BBC.

This recent development thus provides a further opportunity to reflect on the purposes of special programming provision for ethnic minorities and some of the difficulties and dilemmas identified by BBC producers in its production. Part One of this study now turns to those in-house BBC producers involved in the production of special minority ethnic programmes. The interviews for this part of the study were conducted with members of the former Multicultural Programmes Department, now Asian Programme Department, a short time after the announced change. The producers interviewed had previously worked on both Asian and African-Caribbean programmes. While the significance of the recent demise of the Multicultural Programmes Department will be discussed later, the principal focus remains the general viewpoints and experiences of in-house BBC producers and the production of special minority ethnic programmes. The remainder of this chapter will shortly examine the general aims of the former Multicultural Programme Department and its producers before considering, in Chapter Three, the cultural politics of representation that surround and inform producer thinking and programme production practices. Chapter Four next considers various difficulties and constraints identified and confronted by in-house producers working for the BBC. Chapter Five continues this discussion and attends to the institutional nature of the BBC and its internal commissioning processes as experienced and recounted by the producers. Chapter Six finally, and briefly, considers the views of these in-house producers from their particular institutional vantage point on the future of minority ethnic programme production, both general and special, within the BBC.

It is first useful to consider the nature and aims of BBC special programme provision for minority ethnic audiences as these have evolved over the years, up to the present. The following briefly traces this history as outlined by the former Managing Editor of the Multicultural Programmes Department, Narendhra Morar (Morar, 1995). The development of Asian and African-Caribbean programmes can usefully be traced separately.

In respect of Asian programmes the BBC first broadcast programmes aimed specifically at the Asian community in 1965. These programmes were designed to 1) help integrate newly arrived Asian immigrants into their new environment through practical advice; and 2) act as a link with the Indian sub-continent through performances and interviews. The programmes were presented in Hindustani (a hybrid of Hindi and Urdu, the official languages of India and Pakistan respectively). The philosophy informing these programmes was clear in such titles as 'Make Yourself at Home' and 'Naya Zindagee Naye Jeevan' (New Life), produced by the 'Immigrants Unit'. These programmes lacked, according to Morar, hard journalist stories or items of interest to Asian youth. The programmes evolved over the years, arriving at the 'Asian Magazine', a half hour magazine programme broadcast early on Sunday mornings. By the middle of the 1980s the needs and interests of second and third generation Asians were thought not to be catered for by such programmes. As Morar points out, today over 40 percent of the Asian community are third generation most of whom are English speaking. In 1987 revised programming was therefore introduced with 'Network East', a 40 minute magazine typically composed of a mix of journalistic stories, arts and entertainment features presented in English (with interviews sub-titled in English when necessary). In 1988 an Indian drama serial, 'Shrikant' was purchased and broadcast, and in 1989 two of the first documentaries were produced. In 1990 the current affairs element of 'Network East' was separated with the launch of a new series 'East', and the first episodes of the 93 episode saga 'Mahabharat' were broadcast. Themed documentaries followed in 1991. Morar maintains BBC Asian programmes were thus pursuing a four-pronged strategy involving 1) a topical flagship, 'East', broadcast at prime time; 2) an arts and entertainment magazine which is more culturally specific, 'Network East'; 3) documentaries detailing the Asian experience both at home and abroad; and 4) purchased drama serials.

With respect to African-Caribbean programmes, an 'Ebony' production office was first established in Bristol in 1982. This produced a series of half-hour magazine programmes aimed at the African-Caribbean community in Britain. The programme included performance, interviews and short inserts as well as occasional single-subject specials. The first network transmission was in 1982 and by series five the programme was transmitted at prime time on BBC2. In 1985 'Ebony' was moved to Pebble Mill at Birmingham and was discontinued after series eleven. Morar explains: 'The demise of Ebony, the magazine programme, coincided with a change in production philosophy. The magazine format, which involved trying to shoehorn a diversity of items into a single programme, came to be viewed as unsatisfactory because it limited the time and the treatment possibilities for subjects which needed discrete and more substantial treatments' (Morar, 1995, p. 5). Thus, in late 1988 a combination of programmes was produced including documentary one-offs and series, talk shows and location based shows, for example 'Nottinghill Carnival' and 'Ebony on the Road'. A social action philosophy is said to have informed many of these programmes at this time, though black music/entertainment based programmes were also produced. As well as a number of one-off documentaries, major in-house productions across the period 1988 to 1992 included 'Eye to Eye', a documentary series on social issues and individual achievements; 'Under the Skin' a six-part series on South Africa; 'Black Britain', a historical documentary series; 'Black on Europe' a social action documentary series and 'Out of Darkness', a six-part series on pan-African issues. In 1993 the department commissioned a major independent series 'Will to Win' a series of six programmes celebrating black sporting achievement, as well as 'All Black'. This latter series of commissioned programmes tackled hard-hitting issues, such as male prostitution, mental health and the exploitation of illegal immigrants. It attracted controversy for the way in which it handled its selected subjects. A second, less controversial series, ran in 1994.

According to Morar, 'Since the creation of the Multicultural Department as a formal entity, it has begun attempting a programme strategy to more fully reflect the diverse and, indeed, multicultural society that Britain has become ... broadening the department's programme activities to reflect the interests of as many minority communities as possible' (Morar, 1995, p. 7). In line with this new direction an independent company (Juniper) was commissioned to produce 'Nation' a late-night multicultural discussion programme. Further documentaries were commissioned. In addition to the regular series 'East' and 'Network East' a popular studio based quiz on Hindi movies was introduced, 'Bollywood or Bust'; a series on Indian regional cuisine 'Madhur Jaffrey's Flavours of India' was broadcast in 1995 and, also in 1995, major series were commissioned from top Independent companies: 'A Whole Different Ball Game' (Faction Films) revealing new angles on national sports; 'Sadhus' a series on the lives of India's holy men; and 'Ruling Passions: Sex, Race and Empire' (Roger Bolton Productions), a series examining sexual relations between the colonisers and the colonised in India and Africa. In 1995 'African Footsteps' (Diverse Productions) was broadcast, a major series which sought to move away from the famine, dictatorship and disaster agenda and 'instead gives an original and beautifully crafted portrait of Africa in the nineties'.

In summary, the former Managing Editor describes the Multicultural Programme Department as follows:

> The Multicultural Department in 1995 is no longer simply a vehicle for educating ethnic minorities or a hammer with which to bludgeon society's racial problems. Its productions are high profile, mainstream television programmes with wide appeal. In the last year, the department was responsible for over 50 hours of programming, including 19 hours of in-house productions. Some 50% of the programmes are transmitted on Saturday mornings and the remainder on weekday evenings at 19.30 or slightly later. All programmes are broadcast on BBC2.
>
> The Multicultural Programme department has the freedom to move in any direction and to encompass any genre it feels suitable and will do so, always maintaining that production values should be consis-

tently high and that the quality of its output remains above average. (Former Managing Editor, Narendhra Morar, 1995, p. 8)

The brief history of multicultural programming outlined above indicates how minority ethnic programmes have indeed undergone a process of evolution and development. Programmes have been informed, in broad and changing terms, by 'assimilationist', 'race-relations' and 'multicultural' and 'anti-racist' agendas; the volume of programming has generally increased across the thirty year period; the repertoire of 'appropriate' programme subjects has expanded; and the programme formats deployed have become more varied. While these developments, for the most part, can be seen as undoubted gains, the upbeat tenor of the statement is perhaps qualified by the facts presented: 50 hours of programming (less than one hour per week), only 19 hours of in-house productions, 50 percent of programmes transmitted on Saturday mornings, all programmes broadcast on BBC2. The claim that its productions are 'high profile, mainstream programmes' also calls for careful consideration; perhaps some programmes are more 'high profile' than others?; perhaps some are more 'mainstream' than others? What, exactly, constitutes 'mainstream' in contrast to 'special' programmes? Also, in what sense can it be claimed that 'The Multicultural Programmes Department has the freedom to move in any direction and to encompass any genre it feels suitable'? Are we seriously invited to believe there are no limitations or constraints influencing this special provision departments, its producers and programmes? Some of these claims, with the help of in-house producers, will be subject to further scrutiny and discussion over the following pages.

Aims, access and accountability

To begin, however, an explicit statement about basic Department aims is offered by the former Managing Editor:

The basic aims of the Department are to make programmes which contribute to the richness and diversity of the BBC's output, serve those minorities not usually catered for by the other areas of output and provide programming with a distinctive voice, thus enabling the Corporation to more fully reflect the whole of society and justify the licence fee. It also acts as a focus as well as an entry point for people from ethnic minorities, who might not otherwise contemplate the BBC as an organisation in which to make a career. Finally, given that Pebble Mill has been declared a centre of excellence in Multicultural programming, this department can also act as a centre of expertise which other parts of the BBC can draw on. (Morar, 1995, p.2)

Couched in the terms and ethos of multiculturalism, this position on department aims talks about programme 'richness and diversity', 'serv(ing)' minorities, programming with a 'distinctive voice', 'reflect(ing) the whole of society'. It also identifies the possible role of the department in encouraging ethnic minorities to join the BBC and pursue a career there, as well as its value as a source of expertise for other programme makers and departments. In many respects, these basic aims, as we shall hear later, are similar to those advanced by many of the independents reviewed in Part Two; the pursuit of increased access and representation, in the double sense of both 'on' and 'behind' screen, are clearly stated by both. Strategically, these aims are here pursued via a programme department dedicated to the provision of minority ethnic programmes.

It is possible to detect, however, a tension between wanting to provide a service and programming with a distinctive voice aimed at minorities on the one hand, and wanting to be seen as producers of 'high profile', 'mainstream' programmes on the other. While no doubt certain programmes can be both high profile and mainstream, attracting by definition large 'mainstream' audiences, which also appeal to minority ethnic audiences, it is also conceivable that certain minority programmes, if catering to particular needs in their distinctive voices, may not necessarily appeal to large mainstream audiences. Rather than set up an opposition between 'mainstream' and 'minority' programming or try to collapse one into the other, it is perhaps better to recognise the range of programme responses possible between these poles. The producer below appears to recognise as much, but nevertheless insists on being seen, in equal terms, as a 'mainstream' producer:

> Our core brief, speaking as the Multicultural Programmes Department, was to provide programmes that other mainstream programme makers wouldn't provide for the Asian audience and Afro-Caribbean audience. Now that we are the Asian Programme Department again, then obviously it's for the Asian viewers. It's not as if only our department can make programmes that Asians are going to watch, but I think the point is that we can make programmes that Asians in particular are going to find interesting and, depending on the nature of the programme, that a mainstream audience may also find themselves able to take on as well. So our focus is still to make sure that we cater for the Asian audience and then ideally we try and make the programme accessible. (Programme Producer)

But what if the costs of making a programme accessible to a mainstream audience threaten to undermine the internal integrity and coherence of the programme for its identified and intended minority audience? These are difficult and sometimes delicate matters, matters that cannot simply be defined away by suggesting minority programmes are necessarily mainstream, or can easily be accommodated to the mainstream. Listening to the in-house producers, it becomes plain that an institutional struggle for recognition as an equal programme department vis-à-vis other programme departments in the BBC has informed their thinking and practice.

(The department's) first priority should be to make high class production value programmes which anyone in the media would be pleased to have made. That's the bottom line. If you don't make good programmes, we'll be seen as a ghetto, and we cannot afford that sort of label. (Producer/Director)

No longer are Asian programmes considered ghetto programmes; it's more mainstream with budgets comparable to other programme departments within the BBC or ITV. (Producer)

I think people still see us as a kind of ghetto unit that is out there, not within the mainstream of the BBC. I think that our main problem is just changing people's attitudes. But I think that is happening. And we are seen as positive, but I think we need to be seen alongside major BBC departments, which will take a while. (Producer)

No longer are we seen as a ghetto unit, you know, with a kind of sub-standard work. People now want to work on programmes. It just seems like another department within the BBC much more than it was five or ten years ago. (Producer/Director)

One consequence of this claim to equal BBC professional status is manifest, then, in the professional abhorrence of the label 'ghetto programming'. For many this clearly does not signify special minority programming, perhaps deliberately pursued as a temporary but expedient 'enclave strategy', opening doors and opportunities and laying the foundation for more access and competition in the future, but rather conjures up ideas of artificial programme protection, poor quality, small audiences, and generally sub-standard work and a slur upon claims to professionalism. Professionally speaking, such ideas are anathema to the producers' claims to be treated as equals in the

40

rigorously competitive and professional context of BBC television production. Perhaps no wonder they are so reverential towards the idea of the 'mainstream' and are happy see themselves as 'mainstream producers', notwithstanding the fact that they work for a specialist minority programme department. Professional status, competitive claims and perhaps future careers depend upon just such an identification.

Interestingly, when it becomes expedient to extol the virtues and value of a specialised minority programme department, these same producers are quick to point out how, in fact, the 'mainstream' cannot deliver what their department can.

> I think the mainstream's idea of what assimilating Asian people or Afro-Caribbean people into mainstream programming is better than it used to be, but one just needs to look at the way, let's say, the Asians are represented in drama for example. They still seem to have an issue baggage. You rarely see an Asian or an Afro-Caribbean character which doesn't seem to have some kind of issue baggage that they carry around with them as a character. But I think the idea that, because the minority communities are being seen to be more and more visible within mainstream programming, that therefore means there's not a role for minority producers anymore, that's going to be an on-going battle. Unless the industry as a whole, both within the BBC and without it, makes genuine steps to attract and develop talent within the communities there might be a danger that you're not going to get the programme makers. (Producer)

If the producers, for fear of being marginalised as 'ghetto programme makers' in the BBC, have seemed reluctant to identify themselves as producers of special minority programmes, preferring to be seen as professionals working in the so-called 'mainstream', they nonetheless see themselves as apart from and something other than the

41

'mainstream' when it comes to the production of programme representations. Here the 'mainstream' is used as a justification for continued departmental existence. This is not to challenge the validity of the producer's defence of a minority programme department, simply to point out the rhetorical and varied uses that the so-called 'mainstream' can be put to. More important than the producer's conceptual slippage is the way in which a professional claim to equal departmental status internal to the BBC, and perhaps outside it, threatens to detract from the intrinsic value of producing non-mainstream programmes.

If the threat of committing professional suicide were removed, how many BBC producers would aspire to make and transmit programmes that have little or no mainstream appeal? Of course, all writers write to be read, all programmes makers make programmes to be transmitted, but it does not necessarily follow that writers or programme makers must always, necessarily and invariably, produce their products for a mainstream, that is, for a large, predominantly white audience - especially if the deficiencies of the mainstream have prompted their 'special' programme production activities in the first place. As stated above, we are not necessarily dealing with programme opposites but a continuum along which programmes can be differently pitched. Perhaps the point at issue is not so much whether minority programmes shouldn't also be available to the mainstream, that is, large heterogeneous audiences, but the extent to which the aspiration to make programmes for the mainstream unduly influences the production of minority programmes. As the review of programmes produced by the department has indicated, in practice programmes *have* variously been pitched along the continuum of mainstream-minority provision, though to what extent similar variety can be sustained if the 'mainstream' is ever allowed to be the principal arbiter of production is, of course, less certain.

The continuing value and distinctive contribution of special minority programme departments are for the moment acknowledged by all those involved:

This department has a concentrated reserve of experience. There are some very talented people here. This is the one unit where you have perhaps the biggest pool of people who have combined expert, very intense and deep knowledge of Asian culture, Asian affairs are Asian and you can't get any better programme makers than that if you're looking at specific subjects. I've seen programmes which have been made by people, Asian and non-Asian, who have no experience or no idea of what it's really like and their programmes tend to be voyeuristic, very tabloid, very badly researched and very much focused on the negative aspects of the Asian community, in particular in terms of Pakistan and the sub-continent. It would be very bad if you have a lot of uncoordinated independent productions taking over what the department is doing at the moment. (Producer)

We have a sort of history in the department, staff have been built up, we have contacts and so on. I'm not sure that other producers or people elsewhere in the BBC will have that kind of continuity of dealing with the community, that depth of contacts. (Producer)

We have dealt with the community on a longish basis and the programmes have become established. I think that builds up a certain amount of trust within some people because they know it's not a fly by night operation. With other people maybe the programmes have just automatically got a bad name for some reason. They're perceived as some kind of dragons or whatever, so that is a problem. (Producer/Director)

Part of the value of the Multicultural Programmes Department and other special production units, then, is thought to reside in their unique opportunity to build teams of dedicated programme makers who individually and collectively have, or can develop, considerable specialist knowledge in their programme subject areas, and build contacts and trust with minority communities over a period of years. The commitment to increased access and training can also, so it is argued, be sustained only on the basis of specialist departments producing a sufficient volume and range of programming. The Multicultural Programmes Department provided work experience on a routine basis to aspiring programme makers:

> There's a constant, constant stream of work experience people that we have on a regular basis on a two week turn around and I try to make sure that, particularly the best of them, people who really shine when they're here, aren't just ditched and never heard of again ... It's where you come up against departmental programme priorities as a barrier to developing your own staff because again, if you had more output, there would be more to assign people to develop their skills. (Executive Producer)

The provision of training opportunities also provides, according to a department producer, 'another way of keeping in touch with the community, because it's the younger perspectives coming in.' This proves interesting in that it raises the question of representation and the department's 'representativeness' in terms of the wider minority communities and their involvement. Certainly, some producers evidently feel they do help to represent a certain section of their community in so far as their backgrounds, daily circumstances and experiences are similar:

> All the friends I've had, all my family work in and around Heathrow airport so it's a very working class background. It's heavily Asian, Asian populated, everyone we come into contact with in terms of our daily life, our daily life is Asian. In terms of the shops we go to, our friends and neighbours are Asian, all our fami-

lies are obviously around the area. We visit them. There are times during our life where we could go days or weeks without speaking to a white person or a black person unless it's to do with our work. The experience that I contribute to the department is the experience everyday Asians, working class Asians, can relate to. (Producer)

However, and in marked contrast to many of the independent producers and their felt 'organic link' to their communities (discussed in Part Two), BBC producers are here much more wary of assuming, or proclaiming, a representative position. Furthermore, attempts to become too closely involved with any one section of the community is likely to be interpreted as professionally compromising:

> To my knowledge there is not an institutionalised link with the community, though it's the responsibility of the Managing Editors to keep these ties going. But there is always a danger that when these things become too formalised anyway, that inevitably you start getting various interest groups that might start establishing themselves as having the monopoly, and even one's contacts that one maybe keeps in touch with aren't necessarily representative of everybody within the community. (Producer)

Far from a lack of direct 'accountability' to those communities and interests represented within programmes being felt as a possible problem, the claim to professional independence shields the producer from any felt obligation to 'represent'. Or, to put it in other words, programmes broadcast *to* minority communities need not be representative *of* these communities, or even made by programme makers *from* them. While a more interactive, conversational or dialogical approach to multiple community voices can arrive at a similar position of representational pluralism, here the producer's professional stance threatens to minimise any sense of identification whatsoever. Accountability to community interests and groups is thus swept away as if the problem didn't exist.

Summary

The paucity of publicly available information detailing the involvement of ethnic minorities in different roles across the BBC and its corporate hierarchy has been noted and criticised. Without information broken down by different ethnic groups and their involvement in and across different strata of the Corporation, it is impossible to determine whether the numerous public statements of commitment and intent are borne out in practice. While data relating to ethnic minority involvement in programme production appear promising in terms of current levels of involvement, the data clearly remain in need of corporate contextualisation and further sub-division by specified minority groups.

The chapter has also briefly charted the changing nature of the BBC's special provision of multicultural programmes across a thirty year period. The changing aims informing in-house production and commissioning of these programmes across the years have been stated explicitly by the former Managing Editor as have the more recent aims of the Multicultural Programmes, recently separated into the Asian Programmes Department and a more dispersed/flexible arrangement for the production of African-Caribbean programmes. It was observed how, in the broad terms of the pursuit of enhanced representation and access, both on screen and behind screen, the department's aims resonate with broad multiculturalist themes. A concern with encouraging more minority ethnic entrants into the world of television production via the provision of training was a declared aim of both the department and its producers.

A further stated aim was to make good quality, professionally comparable and creditable programmes. This overarching BBC concern with 'production values' was found to have informed the discussion of so-called 'mainstream' and, more pejoratively, 'ghetto programming'. A professional desire to be taken seriously, on equal professional terms by other programme departments and interested parties, appears here to have clouded the distinction between 'mainstream' and 'minority' programmes. With professional status seemingly dependent upon the production of high quality programmes for large 'mainstream audiences', producers have tended to downplay the extent to which some of their programmes are, or should be, deliberately pitched at specific ethnic minority groups and may in consequence have less than widespread appeal. On the other hand, when it came to recognising the limitations of the 'mainstream' in defence of the continued existence of special minority ethnic programme provision, producers here found it useful to differentiate themselves from the mainstream. This conceptual slippage should not be interpreted as simply sloppy thinking but as a professional response to the institutional situation in which producers find themselves. The BBC, after all, is the British Broadcasting (not narrowcasting) Corporation, notwithstanding its more focused stated aims in relation to minorities. Interestingly, though not possible to pursue here, it would prove instructive to attend to the exact institutional definitions of 'British' Broadcasting at play within the Corporation and across its various departments, and how these too may be informed by an 'imagined audience', predefined in relation to assumed characteristics and interests.

The role of special programme departments was understood, perhaps not surprisingly, by all those involved to be a good thing. Specifically, the producers argued that such departments provide an invaluable resource, building teams of dedicated, expert and specialist programme makers who get to know their programme subjects well, building contacts and trust through sustained involvement with communities across the years. Such departments also serve as a focal point for the training of minority ethnic programme makers producing for the BBC and, in time, the television industry more widely. Though here, reference to the low volume of programmes produced was found to impact upon the extent and breadth of training opportunities.

BBC producers have argued how special departments such as the Multicultural or Asian Programmes Department can serve as a resource, a site of accumulated expertise and knowledge, for the BBC as a whole and again for the television industry more widely. Interestingly, in-house producers for the most part did not necessarily feel themselves to be representative, in any organic sense, of the minority communities often the subject of their programmes. Rather, in recognition of the complex interests and heterogeneous nature comprising any so-called 'minority community', as well as a stated professional claim to independence (useful in the competitive environment of programme production as well as the factionalised politics surrounding ethnic and racial affairs), producers tended to eschew any assumed responsibility to be 'representative' in the sense of speaking on behalf of minority ethnic communities or interests and sub-groups therein. Accountability, in the sense of being responsible to programme subjects and represented interests, whether through formal and institutionalised means or more informally through regular discussion and feedback with community interests and groups, appeared not to inform the departments' thinking or practice. Understandably, perhaps, producers working in and for the BBC have sought to secure and maintain professional recognition from their BBC peers and superiors as a credible, professional and, therefore, independent group of programme makers capable of making programmes with high production values for a mainstream audience. In such a context, issues of 'representation' and 'accountability' are likely to become, at best, of secondary importance, at worst, an irrelevance.

3 The cultural politics of representation

As we have heard BBC producers in the Multicultural/Asian Programmes Department have argued, in defence of their own role and department's existence, that they can provide something that other BBC programme departments cannot. The department has publicly declared itself committed to the aim of increasing ethnic minority access both in terms of increased and enhanced representations on screen, as well as providing opportunities for training and involvement in the production of minority ethnic programmes. Inevitably, such a project gives rise to a host of questions. Institutionally and strategically the producers have sought to further their declared aims through the continued existence of a dedicated and specialised ethnic minority programme department. But what exactly do they see as the necessary corrective or additional contribution required of programme representations that the mainstream has failed to provide? What, in other words, do they deem to be the problem at the level of programme representation and what do they aim to put in its place? Questions such as these go the heart of the cultural politics of representation, that contested area in which questions of programme representation and the forms of representation are addressed in relation to the wider play of positions contesting the field of 'race', racism and ethnicity. How do BBC producers position themselves in relation to this surrounding field of contending views and interests? How does their stance inform the representations that they produce? Do they struggle, perhaps, with community-based expectations about the 'proper' nature and role of their programmes? Does their institutional and/or professional position provide a degree of protection from surrounding cultural pressures or does it, perhaps, simply exacerbate them? This chapter sets out to explore these questions relating to the cultural politics of representation. A useful place to begin is with one producer's declared programme aims:

> As an Asian person born and brought up in this country, as an Asian who is truly in touch with his roots and culture, I love my Asian culture and I'm proud of my Asian culture. I don't want it to go undocumented and unseen. I want other people, non-Asians and Asians, to know what's going on. What we're about, where we came from, what we're doing, our aims and achievements, aspirations and our problems. At the end of the day we're people like everybody else, but we have a particular experience and a particular culture which is very different and we should show that and reflect that. It needs to be reflected in television. (Producer)

Here we have an eloquent case for the value and purpose of this form of multicultural programming. Apparently informed by an educational mission directed at non-Asians as much as an informational/cultural purpose in relation to his own community, the producer ignores possible tensions in trying to reach both simultaneously. This generally positive programme celebration of cultural difference says little about how to approach 'difficult' subjects, those issues likely to prove controversial such as, for example, concerns about racism. Where and how should these find representation? A senior in-house BBC producer provides an answer and is in no doubt about what is required if 'the community' is to experience fair television representation:

The only thing that you can do to give the community a fair representation of itself is to provide a range of programmes. It's about volume and it's about range. You can't do it all in six half hour hard-hitting documentary programmes, because they will inevitably dwell on the negative because invariably that's what documentary programmes do, they look at fairly negative things. They don't look at all the things to celebrate. Other types of programmes, Arts and Entertainment, do. Drama might. I'm very conscious that having something the community will relate to means giving a range of programmes, it means having enough programmes on air for it to be a regular feature for people to tune in and it also means having enough types of programmes to really accurately reflect the range of experiences inside a community. Otherwise you will inevitably end up subbing it all down to a problem and another problem and another problem on your factual programme series. (Executive Producer)

This more pluralistic view of representation as conditional upon both volume and range of programmes offers an implied solution to the so-called problem of the 'burden of representation'. In recent years the phrase 'the burden of representation' has been used to describe the additional responsibility felt by black producers who, confronted by too few opportunities to make and show their films and programmes, feel an obligation to use each and every opportunity to counter dominant media representations. On behalf of their wider communities and their expectations, producers thus carry a heavy representational responsibility - a pressure not experienced by their white counterparts. Here the solution to such a problem appears clear, and involves considerations of both volume and range. Both volume and range of programmes are needed in order to permit 'hard-hitting' journalistic pieces because only then can such 'negative' representations be balanced by the weight of other programmes with their more varied and 'positive' portrayals. The producer's claim that some programme forms are inherently disposed towards the 'negative' can be qualified however. Though it may well be the case that current affairs or documentary genres have often been deployed to examine and expose the contentious issues or concerns of public (*and* private) life, there is nonetheless more flexibility in their respective subject treatments than the producer's simple description of 'negative' suggests. How subjects are treated, as much as what subjects are selected, are concerns that cannot necessarily be reduced to the automatic predispositions of a genre. Television genres are not fixed but evolve and develop through time, as the increasingly hybrid forms of *infotainment* television programmes demonstrate. A certain genre *and* medium determinism nonetheless informs the statements of programme makers:

> We submit ideas and we try to go from looking at black stereotypes and doing something more positive, but I think in television, in newspapers the negative side usually appeals rather than looking at the positive, which is the way it will always be. (Researcher)

The overriding aim of the BBC producers is not simply to replace 'negative' with 'positive' images, however, but to provide multiple views on minority ethnic communities and affairs, in all their complexity and ordinariness:

> I would like there to be enough of a range of programming to enable people like me to make tough programmes without making a one-sided statement. I'd like to see these communities in all their aspects on the tele. Not just when they're sportsmen, not just when they're entertainers making people laugh. Not just when they're victims and villains but all the incidental stuff. I'd like to see them cropping up incidentally when they just happen to be black on a drama... Just let them find script-writers who know how black and Asian people operate, but don't turn them into issues

every time they're on television. You know, integrate them in the way that people are integrated. Black people don't spend their whole time talking about being black. They go to Tescos, they make dinner, they do their homework, they draw their pensions, they do all those really banal things everyone else does, so that's where they need to be shown. And on top of that, yes, there are experiences and aspects of being black in Britain which are always at risk of being overlooked. Yes racism, yes immigration, yes all the big issues which aren't going away; we can't afford to fall silent on them. But we've got to find new ways of saying old things and I think that's the responsibility of good programme makers. (Executive Producer)

Aware of the value to broaden, and perhaps deepen, programme representations, the producers did not feel diffident about tackling 'difficult' or revelatory subjects, subjects that many audience members may simply interpret as adding fuel to the slow-burning embers of 'negative' television portrayal. Interestingly, this was not simply to do with the balancing impact of a wider range of programmes, but related to the professional way in which potentially controversial and/or damaging subjects were handled. The Executive Producer explains at some length:

I think there are a lot of liberals who have probably given anti-racism a bad name precisely because sometimes anti-racism, or not wanting to be seen to be racist, has turned them into being mealy mouthed and being dishonest and not tackling subjects honestly and properly. And I think you've got to be smart enough to steer a course ... Programme makers do need to have a conscience and then to listen to their consciences and their gut instincts. I'm not in the school of thought that says 'Do whatever you think and don't listen to your conscience', not at all. But I do think when you make a programme, you have to be conscious of what consequences that programme will have on the community, or the people or the individuals on that programme. And when you know that the bulk of the imagery of say, the Afro-Caribbean community involves them looking pretty poor, ragged, aggressive, if not criminal, then you have to be conscious of that. So that's the context within which you make programmes.

If you want to tackle a problem like single mothers, like single parents who are in the Afro-Caribbean community, you do it. But it's a question of how you contextualise it. What I object to are the programmes that are unkind and it's very difficult to describe 'unkind' until you hear it. Unkind is when you hear facts bandied about and things that divide the community in a way that you think, well, for anyone who knows that community, that doesn't feel right. That doesn't feel like the people I've met, and I'm not just being protective towards them. I'm just saying that actually doesn't reflect the whole range of experience inside the community. So I think you have to be careful because there's a lot of ignorance. You don't want to compound the ignorance. You don't want to confirm people's worst suspicions. So you've got to do something to say, 'here's a problem' and find a way of contextualising which doesn't make all the old ladies in middle England buy another bolt for their door because they think black people are coming to get them. And you can do that. So often it's a question of tone and knowing your subject matter and giving the kind of interviews that turn people into human beings rather than 'public enemy number one'.

And that really is about getting people to open up in front of the camera and how you edit it, and how you contrast things. (Executive Producer)

Here the 'burden of representation' is, to some extent, apparently lightened by producers being aware of the predominant television imagery, being informed about their subject matter and subject community, and providing contextualisation in their programme treatments and thereby undermine possible racist responses. Clearly, the producer does feel an obligation to challenge possible racist interpretations of her programme subjects. Like her colleagues above, then, the Executive Producer does not assume a position of 'community representative', though arguably she appears to entertain a position of professional omniscience in so far as programmes aim to 'contextualise' programme subjects in ways that are assumed to be valid and beyond dispute. While some viewpoints are more adequate than others, and those of specialist programme makers may well be informed by considerable experience and understanding, there is no guarantee that the programme maker's interpretation inscribed into the structure of his/her programme escapes the partial, or even partisan, assumptions and outlook of a particular viewpoint. To assume otherwise is to succumb to the myth of disinterested journalism. The fact that the producer is only too aware of how certain subjects can lend support to racist viewpoints and seeks ways of disarming them in practice, suggests that she does carry a certain 'burden' on behalf of an anti-racist and/or multicultural stance - a stance that is directed outwards towards the wider white community. Once again, then, programmes directed at mainstream, white audiences are informed by an obligation to counter dominant myths and assumptions about racial minorities. The producer's programme stance in relation to the cultural politics of representation thus appears to be informed by a blend of the professional and the political. It is also heavily informed by the pragmatic:

The most important thing for minority ethnic programme makers is to get a good job in television and don't worry too much about being part of something that you perhaps don't fully approve of. Because, until people are in a position of power, they can't control exactly how things are made and what they say. If you're a researcher inevitably you will see some of your research turned in directions you don't like. That's par for the course. But you've got to stick in there doing enough to get up the greasy pole. Get the experience, bite your tongue and do what every other programme maker does which is get the experience under your belt. Then, when you've got pips on your shoulder, then you can start calling the tune. Obviously, try and make programmes you are proud of. Obviously, say your piece but don't feel you can carry the burden of representing your community on your shoulders because you can't, you can't, you won't survive. You won't survive in this climate in the television industry in that way, because people don't have enough respect for what you see as your responsibility and you've got to live with that. Because otherwise you won't get through. I think that's important. Programme makers have got to stick in there and not get demoralised and frustrated by not seeing their views represented in ways that they want, until they've got the chance to work for someone who is sympathetic or has enough authority to be able to say, 'Well this is how we'll do it, and not that way.' (Executive Producer)

Here we have the views of an experienced, senior BBC producer on the cultural politics of representation. Claims are not made about representing the community - 'the community' is too diverse and differentiated for that; nor are *express* political commitments at work. Rather, 'representation' becomes a matter of programme volume and range; only then can expression be given to the full complexity and differences found within and across minority communities. So-called 'difficult' and possibly controversial subjects are not eschewed, though these need to be handled professionally. That is, they need to be handled sensitively; their subject matter needs to be contextualised and situated within a carefully constructed programme design - a programme design that denies support to popular racist myths. This blend of the professional approach to programme making, informed by a deep-seated abhorrence of racism, is also tempered, as we have just heard, with an institutional pragmatism experienced in the art of personal and professional survival. Why, exactly, this pragmatism has come about within the BBC will be explored in the following chapters.

Also informing this professional stance to the cultural politics of representation is an encompassing view of 'multiculturalism' or, to turn it around, a less than committed stance to any one community group, minority faction *or* informing politics. Many of the in-house producers, for example, expressed interest in pushing beyond the conventional and BBC identification of multiculturalism as more or less confined to Asian and African-Caribbean groups and cultures:

> I think the term multicultural is used too narrowly in this country and the BBC. We are only exploring the Asian sub-continent and Afro-Caribbean (sic), so what about China? What about South America? What about the South Pacific? What about Japan? Don't all these come under the term multicultural as well? I think our brief should be much, much broader. (Producer)

> Certainly the BBC's conception of multicultural programming has generally been African-Caribbean. I think it would be nice to see someday a multicultural current affairs series that spreads out to encompass the whole variety of different cultures that live in Britain from orthodox Greeks to whatever. We haven't really done anything for the oriental community, for example, in this country. Quite how that's going to happen now in the future without a Multicultural Programmes

57

Department I'm not sure. But I think that would be one of the ways in which the programming could have moved forward. To widen its ambit beyond the two, if you like, core communities. (Producer)

There's a hell of a lot more communities under the umbrella of 'multicultural' or 'ethnic minorities'. They're generally not seen on television. Their programming is completely left out so in that direction there is a completely open market for whoever wants to delve into that. (Researcher)

This position, though laudable as a generalised future multicultural aim, fails to appreciate some of the distinctive differences relating to Asian and African-Caribbean minorities and their contemporary experiences and conditions of existence in Britain, in contrast to those of other minority groups. The term 'minority' after all is not simply a numerical designation, but typically refers to imbalances of economic, political and social power, inequalities forged in relation to a colonial past, diaspora movements and histories, and contemporary patterns of disadvantage, discrimination and cultural adjustment. Multiculturalism has always needed to pursue more than a celebration of difference if it is to engage with the lived experiences of minority groups. In the comments above it would appear that the producers' general appreciation of cultural difference, in terms of a kind of 'multicultural equivalence', threatens to underestimate the very real *political* differences of history, patterns of inequality and cultural engagement that have characterised the experiences and responses of particular minority groups. The extent to which a position of *multicultural equivalence* informs producer thinking, that is, a position which seemingly ignores considerations of structural inequality and imbalance between (dominant) ethnic groups and minority ethnic groups, is graphically illustrated in the following:

I would like to make it very clear, I'm not into the idea of making Asian programmes made only by Asian people. I think it should be a two way thing. If you live in a community, especially where there is a white majority, you need white people to work with you. I would loathe the idea of Asian programmes only made by Asian people. Because it doesn't do anyone any good. It segregates. You can't have it both ways: Asians or Afro-Caribbeans saying I want to go and work in the news, I want to go and work in documentaries, I want to go and work in drama. You can't say that on the one hand, and then say 'Oh, by the way Asian programmes, Afro-Caribbean programmes should only be made by them'. (Producer/Director)

Of course, it is possible to object that it is perfectly reasonable and understandable for British Asians or African-Caribbeans to want to gain access to the full spectrum of programme departments while maintaining privileged status and access to designated special Asian and African-Caribbean programme production. The programme playing field as presently constituted is not one of multicultural equivalence, but is historically and institutionally weighted towards dominant groups - a motivating factor for the setting up of special programme provision in the first place.

Summary

BBC in-house producers have expressed a range of views on the cultural politics of representation. While some clearly entertain a positive multicultural faith in the necessity for all communities to be exposed to, and learn about, different minority cultures, when it comes to the representation of 'difficult' or contentious community issues and affairs, differences of approach have been noted. In-house producers have declined the role of community 'representative'. Not that they do not feel an obligation to counter dominant stereotypical images and unduly negative television agendas. Their response to the 'burden of representation', however, has involved a twin representational politics: firstly, to push for more volume of programming and range of representations, thereby balancing and to some extent off-setting the impact of expose and controversial subjects; and, secondly, to produce programmes informed by a developed professionalism - a stance that declines to adopt and champion a particular viewpoint while nonetheless providing valid contextualisation to programme subjects in order to deny support to racist interpretations.

While producer professionalism to some extent appears to lighten the burden of representation, producers cannot assume a position of detachment or omniscient understanding of their subject matter and remain caught-up in the play of contending viewpoints and perspectives. The recognition of dominant stereotypes and racist motifs also compels producers to challenge these within their programme treatments, indicating how programmes in practice are produced with at least one eye firmly on the white audience - perhaps a further concession to producing programmes for the mainstream. BBC producers have also indicated a pragmatic response to the institutional conservatism of the BBC itself, and developed a defensive posture to programme design and production at least until gaining positions of responsibility. This blend of the professional, political and the pragmatic arguably makes for a distinctive in-house producer approach to programme subjects, an approach that will be contrasted later to those often more engaged, expressly political and less disinterested programme ambitions of many of the independents interviewed in Part Two.

Some of the in-house producers also gave expression to what was here called *'multicultural equivalence'*, a seeming appreciation of minority groups and cultural differences as intrinsically worthy of equal programme attention. Such a position, it was argued, fails to fully appreciate the historical, structural and systematic inequalities and differences that inform different minority experiences and cultures and therefore fails to recognise the strategic validity of pursuing both privileged access to special programme production *and* increased representation within general programme production across departments.

4 Controls, constraints and limitations

In the preceding chapters a number of producers' comments made reference to their institutional position within the BBC and how this has affected their programme production and outlook. This chapter, and the next, pursue issues of institutional control, constraints and other limitations more closely. Producer accounts and reflections on their relation to the institutional ethos and production environment of the BBC, the minority communities which they seek to serve, and the internal 'gatekeepers' or decision-makers within the BBC form the principal foci of discussion. This chapter thus attends to considerations of general BBC ethos and production context, as well as the difficulties experienced in seeking to reach complexly differentiated community audiences. The following chapter takes up, and pursues further, concerns of control in relation to internal gatekeeping and decision-making.

The BBC in-house producers interviewed generally painted a picture of the BBC as a relatively exclusive, staid and unadventurous programme-making environment, an environment impacting upon particular social groups and minority ethnic programme makers particularly:

> I feel the mainstream BBC, although there's the equal

opportunity policy, I think there's still a lack of opportunities for minorities to get into mainstream media. It's easy to feel scared to kind of walk into the newsroom or walk into features, it's tough. You're kind of dealing with very well established, white, male middle-class attitudes and you can feel you don't belong to that club. It's hard to break into it, and that's a major problem. And I would go so far as saying, that's not just a major problem for minorities, it's a major problem for white working class people. (Producer/Director)

If the BBC is experienced as a relatively exclusive, white male, middle-class dominated club, an overwhelming ethos of conservatism is also found to impact upon programme design and production:

> I just feel sometimes that we cop out and that we water down; we are just not aggressive, perhaps that's the wrong word, but we're just not progressive in exploring the issues facing our community purely because we are scared of the backlash we would face. Because there's not many Asian programmes on TV, our department is the focus and it has the most physical profile so we have to be very careful. So I can understand the attitude. And also, you know, we work for the BBC as well. We have to be very careful. (Producer)

The Producer above reveals how programme design can be informed by a certain timidity in anticipation of potential reaction both from the programme audience and the BBC itself. Apparently this is more than the unavoidable difficulty of the 'burden of representation' mentioned earlier, where audiences carry high, and sometimes unrealisable, expectations of 'their' programmes and are likely, therefore, to criticise loudly when they feel they have been poorly served. The problem is *also* laid firmly at the door of the BBC. The BBC, *sui generis*, is a cautious institution. Furthermore, this institutional ethos of conservatism is observed to have impacted upon programme innovation at the level of form as well as subject matter. Discussing an independent's 'innovative' programme one producer commented:

> At the BBC, because of the kind of staidness and the very fact that sometimes it is not very willing to experiment, not willing to be daring, something like that would just be deemed, 'Oh well, that's not really quite what we do here'. It would have been deemed too experimental, too daring. (Producer)

If minority programme makers experience a prevailing ethos of programme conservatism and feel constrained to work within this, some also experience a lingering racism in their dealings with technical and support staff. Not only is this in direct contradiction to declared BBC aims and equal opportunity policies, it also, of course, impacts directly upon production decisions and practices:

> There's still a lot of institutionalised and underground racism, especially from technical staff. I have always felt very uncomfortable, even when I was in research and starting to direct, about using BBC technical staff in the form of editors and soundmen, dubbing editors, cameramen. I've always felt there has been a certain resentment and a certain feeling that we're just a joke. That we're not serious, that we make crap programmes and we're crap. I feel this is still continued inside the BBC. Personally, because of 'Producer Choice', I'm very glad that we can go outside. I don't want to go outside, I want to stay and cut all my items, to use BBC resources. I want a job and I want other people in the BBC to have a job because then their future's secure, my future's secure. But when you're faced with that situation - I'm born and brought up in this country and I know, I have a sixth sense. All Asians develop a

63

sixth sense; you know when somebody is being racist, no matter how nice they are, you know if somebody is racist. You know if someone doesn't like you purely because of what colour you are. You know that and nobody can turn round and say to me, 'Oh, I'm not being racist, nothing against you'. Because I know that. I can detect it and I know. And so you feel very angry and very bitter about going downstairs. You want things done. They don't do things for you, or they come up with excuses; the way they talk to you, they just make you feel like a piece of dirt. And this attitude has been prevailing. It's not everyone; there are people down there who are nice; there are people in the BBC who are nice. Technical staff who are nice. Who you can talk to, who are understanding. But I think this has been a big drawback, which is one reason why we go outside. Why I don't feel bad about using the outside crews. (Producer)

The producer's decision to make full use of 'Producer Choice', the system by which producers can 'shop around' both inside and outside the BBC for their programme inputs and services, has clearly been informed, in this instance, by a perception of racist BBC technical support staff. If this has impacted directly upon production decisions and also technical support (it is not so practicable or convenient to involve outside parties in follow-up support), it has also contributed to the perceived climate of special minority ethnic programme making as a 'ghetto' activity with all the pejorative associations, discussed earlier, for producers and their claims to equal professional respect. Here, however, the idea of 'ghetto' programming, apparently held by at least some technical support staff, becomes a fully racialised stigmatisation.

Not that everything is criticised at the BBC. Producers also acknowledged some of the positive advantages of working for this established public-service institution:

Well there are things that you can do, because you can

pick up the phone and say 'BBC' and immediately people make assumptions. Sometimes those assumptions are awful, like they think you've got a really big budget. That you can afford to give them loads of money because it's a rich organisation and in fact they don't realise that you've got a tiny budget and you can't afford to give them fifty quid or one hundred quid, or two hundred quid or three hundred quid for whatever it is they're doing. The good side is the instant recognition. No matter where you go, no matter who you speak to, there's a certain element of respect for you as a programme maker. But when you say, 'I'm from Fulcrum Production' or 'I'm from Independent Productions' they say 'Who?' So that's nice. You're the same person, but suddenly the word 'BBC' gives you an automatic respectability. (Executive Producer)

Advantages are not confined to external public respect for the BBC however, but also relate to the stability the BBC can offer, the prevalence of other producers and the availability of their expertise, and other sources of support all of which can only be provided by a large television organisation:

I like being in large buildings where there are a lot of programme makers making programmes. I think that should give you a buzz. It's much nicer than working out of some ramshackle, makeshift office, which only exists as long as your programme is being made. So it's the fact that it's here and it's always here and you come in and out of it and it's regular and solid and stable. It gives you an air of stability. A lot of the people who work here know the system. There's a system, there are ways of doing things. Again it takes time to learn them, but when you understand them, it does mean that you're not starting from scratch every time you work on a programme. You know, you make contacts with editors downstairs. You find out who the best ones are. They're around; you can get them back again. These are things that are really, really useful. So all that is good. Like I say, there are so many things the BBC could do better, so many and if only they would stop worrying, and if only they would stop talking to themselves and if only they would just enact things rather than produce glossy brochures on them. (Executive Producer)

Producers also have to deal with community perceptions of the BBC which are often less than positive. This is not just a matter of wrestling ideologically with the felt 'burden of representation', but also a *practical* difficulty that has to be confronted when seeking to involve certain community voices and viewpoints into their programmes:

I think we do a pretty good job of it, but the hardest thing is, as I mentioned earlier, the public's perception of the BBC in general. I think it holds us back ... When we first started doing 'Bollywood or Bust', which is a quiz show from here, people didn't believe that the BBC were actually making a quiz show for the Asians - they couldn't believe it. They sometimes have this view of the BBC being this institution full of horrible men in grey suits, predominantly a white establishment kind of place, and they are quite shocked that you're from the BBC, and whenever I'm out filming they all think we're from TV Asia or ZTV. (Researcher)

It means that you don't walk into a room and when you say BBC, everyone's eyes light up and they go, 'Oh brilliant, you've come to make some programmes'! They say, 'Oh, the BBC. What do they want?' And you say, 'Well look, I know I'm from the BBC' and you do this sort of 'I understand what you're saying and I've come into the department to try and do something about it and what do *you* want to do about it?' And so it takes persuading, but again, you get a track record. (Executive Producer)

There is also the added practical difficulty of trying to involve participants on programmes that other members of the community may feel should not be made, perhaps either because of community insularity or community insecurity vis-à-vis prevalent white assumptions and viewpoints about their communities:

> People will often say things off camera to you. You could do a great deal of research and spend up to two hours talking to them and they'll say all these things. But stick a camera on them in the studio full of fifty people and it becomes a bit problematic. There is the fear of television, but the fear of the community also on certain issues. There is a kind of belief, I think personally, amongst Asians that you shouldn't put out your dirty linen in public, and to keep it within the community and sort it out amongst ourselves. Obviously the whole nature of television is in direct contradiction to that and that's where problems can come. (Producer)

Differences of response from different communities are also recounted by producers, and related to the profile of the BBC's special *and* general programme output:

> Asian audiences I think have some reason to be quite pleased with the range of output, though there might be a case for more volume. There might be a case for more range, but you can see that it's moving in the right direction. The Afro-Caribbean audience is so, so negative about the BBC that it's become cynical to the

point where it's like, 'Well of course the BBC doesn't
have anything for us. They aren't interested in what
we say. They are only interested in us when we are
committing crimes or are the victims of crime.' And
that's what you come up against. (Executive Producer)

The acknowledged disparity between Asian and African-Caribbean
programming produced by the Multicultural Programmes Department
will be addressed further below. Here it becomes clear that producers
also feel they have to struggle with the complexities and differences
that characterise the so-called 'Asian community'. While in one
sense, community complexity helps fragment the producers' 'burden
of representation' by dispersing obligations across a wide range of
community groups and factions - so many, in fact, that it may prove
unrealistic to entertain expectations that they could all find adequate
representation. In another sense, community complexity and differences present producers with a challenge, especially if some communities are more geared-up than others to the ways of the media:

We can't say 'what do you want us to make' directly.
We don't want the community to dictate what we can
do, but at the same time we can take account of what
they want from us. The key problem is breaking down
the Asian community within itself. I think the Muslim
community, especially the Bengali and to some extent
the Sri Lanken community, feel they have really been
left out. They feel it's dominated by Hindi/Indian
against Pakistani/Muslim. I have to admit last year's
'Network East', though we tried to balance out Hindi
or Islamic/non-Islamic stories, when it comes to doing
stories about the Bengali community in this country,
there are very few stories there. The Bangladeshi
community is not experienced in dealing with the
media. The classic example is some star came early
this year. If he was someone from the Asian community, some promoter would have rung us or we would

have found out because word gets around, for whatever reason. A Bangladeshi star has come and the only
time you might hear about it is when they are already
gone. We even asked the High Commission, we talked
to people in the community: 'why didn't you give us a
call?', because we can't always keep up to date about
where everybody is. (Producer/Director)

Not only are there complex differences of religion, language and
region of family origin to contend with, there are also generational
differences and continuing animosities. Importantly, these animosities
are said to have impacted upon the selection and treatment of programme subjects:

One of the major problems which has existed in the
past, and still exists to a degree, is the division between
religious factions and also racial factions as well.
Since partition in 1947, you've always had some en-
mity between Indian and Pakistanis and that is still the
case amongst the older generation. The forty plus
generation who remember partition, who remember
the pain of separation, who remember all the battles
and struggles. There are Muslims who will only shop
at Muslim shops and hate Indian Hindus and Sikhs
with passion; likewise you will get Sikhs who do not
like Muslims. And the problem we've had in facing
that in 'Network East' is that we've been scared,
especially since you take the Salman Rushdie affair;
we always feel that Muslims feel they are getting a raw
deal, getting a very bad deal from the press and TV in
general. So we've always been very, very careful,
especially in our coverage of Muslim/Pakistani affairs,
because of the trouble it can lead to. For example, with
our editor and our department, we feel we can't cover
specific religious events. The reason being, that if we
covered one which falls in our programme span which

69

is October to December, how do we cover Ede which
falls in April when we're not on air? (Producer)

Again, it would appear that lack of programme volume, now measured
in terms of seasonal programming, and when set alongside producers'
sensitivities to their audiences' differences and animosities, under-
mines the possibility of dealing with different community festivals and
events. Examples of programme 'silences' do not only concern seasonal community festivities, however, but extend to 'big' journalistic
stories. These too can be affected by the lack of continuous all-year-
round programming:

> It would be great to be all the year round. I don't think
> we actually hit the fuse sometimes, because we're only
> on ten weeks of the year, and when something kicks
> off, for example the recent trouble in Bradford, we
> weren't on air. We didn't have airtime to cover it and
> those are the kind of things that we should be respond-
> ing to and should be covering, but we just haven't got
> the airtime. (Researcher)

Further examples of subjects deemed potentially controversial to
different minority communities and thus ignored, are provided by the
producer. Unlike the examples above, however, these programme
silences cannot simply be explained with reference to the seasonal run
of certain programmes, but are accounted for by senior producers'
unwillingness to provoke possible hostile reactions:

> There are some Rap groups, militant Asian Rap
> groups, coming up who take a lot of pride in their
> Muslim roots, in their Pakistani roots and in their
> Muslim religion. How can we show them? There is a
> thin line between their acceptance of the religion and
> the way they deride it. If we show them with these
> controversial lyrics, we will offend certain members of
> the Pakistani community, the Muslim community.

70

How do we get round that? This has been a major point. I believe firmly we should do them. We should do something on them to show where they are coming from and how this is a new face of Asian youth. A militant, aggressive kind of stance. But there would be problems with the editorial management taking the line that their lyrics are very controversial for attacking the white race or white imperialists of the past. I feel personally that, even though I disagree with them, as a journalist we should be showing that this is the feeling of people, this is what they are saying. So we have to be very careful and it is a problem. There are certain people we can't cover, certain subjects we can't cover purely because of the problems we may face. (Producer)

It appears that a recognition of, and sensitivity towards, inter-minority community differences combined with BBC conservatism and timidity to narrow the types of subjects deemed acceptable for programme representation. With these final producer observations, the discussion is returned once again to how the institutional nature of the BBC impacts upon programme output. The following chapter now pursues this, and other considerations, in its discussion of BBC gatekeepers and decision-makers.

Summary

This chapter has begun to examine some of the major constraints and limitations identified by producers in their professional practice when making ethnic minority programmes. The institutional nature of the BBC, described by one producer as a relatively exclusive club composed predominantly of white, middle-class males, has contributed to a programme production ethos characterised by conservatism and timidity. This has influenced programme makers who feel unable to innovate in matters of form or pursue certain subjects deemed potentially too controversial. This BBC conservative ethos, said to permeate the institution as a whole, has proved particularly debilitating to producers of minority ethnic programmes. Unfortunately, according to at least some of the producers interviewed, lingering racism also continues within some of the technical support departments of the BBC and has contributed to producers going outside the Corporation for their programme support services. This explicit form of crude racism, however, appears to be confined to certain sections of the Corporation and is clearly at odds with the BBC's public pronouncements on equal opportunities et cetera. As we have seen, the major difficulties and stumbling blocks confronting producers of minority ethnic programmes are thought to relate less to racisim and more to the established working traditions, the social composition of the BBC, its institutional hierarchy and programme production conservatism.

On the other hand, certain advantages are also provided by the BBC. As a large programme producer and broadcaster of long-standing, the BBC offers producers benefits in the world of programme production including: the provision of a stable base from which to work - by no means a universal condition for many producers; a busy environment in which expertise and support can readily be found; and, in some contexts at least, the mantle of respectability afforded by the BBC's wider public reputation. That said, the public face of the BBC, as far as the producers experienced it, did not generally commend them to potential programme participants drawn from minority groups and communities. In fact, they related how they have had to struggle to overcome past and continuing community disappointments and/or unrealistic expectations of the BBC and its programme representations. Here different responses by black and Asian audiences were observed, and the intra-community differences and complexities characterising the so-called 'Asian community' acknowledged. Community insularities and/or community insecurities possibly account for some of the less than equal involvement of different ethnic minority communities in special programming provision, as well as differing degrees of community-media contact. Also contributing to programme subject treatments and programme omissions are producer sensitivities towards intra-community animosities and divisions.

72

When combined with the informing BBC culture of programme conservatism this has resulted, according to the producers, in certain subjects deliberately remaining untouched. The less than continuous nature of special programme provision has also resulted in producers not being able to respond to certain events and issues if and when they occur. Once again, the 'burden of representation', as professionally experienced, relates to considerations of both the quantity and quality of television's programme representations.

5 Commissioners, gatekeepers and sweethearts

At first it may appear strange to have a chapter about in-house producers entitled 'Commissioners, gatekeepers and sweethearts'; after all, these are usually discussed in terms of the relationship of dependency of outsiders upon insiders. The relationship between independents and commissioning organisations is certainly a key interface where, as discussed later in Chapter Ten, independents must learn to negotiate with, and fathom the latest schedule needs and commissioning aims of, institutional gatekeepers. However, this relationship also exists internal to broadcasting organisations, the BBC included, and is therefore potentially of considerable interest in our efforts to understand the controls, constraints and limitations shaping in-house production of ethnic minority programmes. This chapter turns, therefore, to the institutional context of the BBC and attends to producers' accounts and experiences of programme production, now with a particular interest in internal commissioning and the subsequent decision-making which shapes the producers' programmes. It also examines, from the inside as it were, some of those issues raised later when discussing commissioning processes in relation to independent producers. Senior in-house producers are well-placed to comment upon and provide possible insights into the processes of commissioning of independents and the prevalence of so-called 'sweetheart' deals. When involved in commissioning the producer 'poacher' becomes the institutional gatekeeper or 'gamekeeper' and offers a different vantage point on the commissioning process.

The problem of BBC institutional conservatism, raised in the last chapter, is here clearly of continuing concern in so far as it colours the relationship between minority ethnic producers and more senior corporate decision-makers. The nature of the predominantly white, male, middle-class culture of the BBC is experienced as unproductive, and on occasion unhelpful, in terms of facilitating professional communication and understanding:

> It's things like, just talking from my own experience, the experience of walking into a room full of executives of the BBC in this building (Pebble Mill, Birmingham) and they're all men and they're all big and tall and white. They're all having a nice time, and you walk in and you join one of the groups and there is no hostility or anything like that, it's just the fact that they're talking business and they turn round and they say, 'Have you got a new haircut?' And I say, 'I haven't got a new haircut', you know! You'd think, you know, I'm an Executive Producer, I'm 33, I make programmes and yet they think all they can talk to me about is my haircut. Why? And you don't want to overreact and say, 'Don't be so patronising', because they won't understand what you mean. So you're constantly trying to fight this irritation with people who, with the best will in the world, don't respond to you in the way that they should. (Executive Producer)

The conservatism of the BBC is not thought to simply inhere in the social composition of senior decision-makers, however, but is also traced to the rigid bureaucratic structures of the corporation. These are experienced, as described in detail below, as hindering the flow of communication and impacting upon the producer's capacity to innovate and push forward new programme ideas with confidence and a sense of institutional support:

> The people who have been here for ten years don't act like the programme makers I know, because they've got into that institutionalised civil service mentality that the BBC engenders at its worst ... I have been incredibly frustrated ever since I set foot in the BBC. Prior to this I worked for Channel Four, and Channel Four has a lot of faults but it is accessible. Everybody in Channel Four is accessible. If you want to speak to anybody, pick up the phone to them. In the BBC you have such an intense sort of Byzantine bureaucracy in operation that it is deemed totally outrageous to pick up the phone to anyone who isn't your immediate superior because it is seen as disrespecting your head of department. So as a result, the programme controller, who is the man who commissions our programmes, is someone that I have never, ever, had the opportunity of speaking to, and that drives me mad. As an executive producer I need to know what the person who is buying my programmes thinks of them, and I need to know what he's got in mind. Not because I'm going to give him everything he wants, but because that's how programme making works. You find out what they want, you have an idea and you meet somewhere in between. That never happens, and for me that is the most annoying thing. I spend most of my time saying why can't we talk to Michael Jackson (BBC2 Controller)? Why can't even my head of department speak to Michael Jackson directly? He has to go to the Head of Network Television Midlands and East, who would then take it to Michael Jackson. So by the time it got back to me it was gobbledegook. That was a big, big problem. To this day I don't know what perception Michael Jackson has of me, my pro-

grammes, and I've had no opportunity to talk to him about the kind of ideas I would like to put forward. (Executive Producer)

Lack of communication, inhibited by 'Byzantine bureaucracy' and rigid hierarchy, is thus said to impact upon the commissioning process, with the programme producer forced, in the absence of engaged dialogue, to guess the latest senior decision maker's thinking on programme requirements. A point further confirmed in the following:

So I feel that there are times when I've wasted my time trying to fulfil briefs that have changed by the time that they get back to the person who has requested them. And that's the biggest lesson I've learnt: go on your own gut instincts because if you trust the judgement of other people, the problem is that you don't know what they're basing their judgements on and, if they change, then you're left thinking, 'Well I didn't want to do that anyway, ... What has been a major constraint for me has been the frustration of not getting new programmes on the air. That has been a major constraint. Not being able to have a dialogue with the person who commissions. (Executive Producer)

The hierarchical and bureaucratically remote nature of the BBC is thus said to impact upon the commissioning process and contributes to the conservatism of programme production. Again, an unfavourable comparison has been drawn with Channel Four:

In terms of Channel Four versus the BBC, I've got to say the BBC is much more conservative. You've got to jump through a lot more hoops generally to get a programme on the air and it shows. There are too many people employed to sort of rub their chins and then say 'Um...not sure about that'. The number of people who need to see a tape prior to transmission,

77

particularly if it's deemed politically sensitive. Utterly understandable, but it creates an atmosphere. There are two ways to approach programmes. One is to say, 'We've got to make sure it's right'. And the other is to say, 'Have a go and let's see what we can do'. And the former is the BBC and the latter is how we worked at Channel Four. (Executive Producer)

A different producer draws a similar comparison, referring to how the BBC's rigid management structure inhibited programme experimentation and innovation:

Sometimes the ideas are too outlandish because of cost. But when you look at some of the things Channel Four does, one thing I admire about Channel Four and the independent structure is that they have a free hand to do anything. Sometimes it works, sometimes it doesn't work. But still they try. I think it's better to have a badly made programme and do one run, a badly made experimental programme in terms of editorial content, visual style, and do one run rather than not run it at all. Because we're locked into a permanent title of 'Network East' it gives very little room for experimentation, and also we have a management structure here which is very strong, very rigid and a lot of ideas and concepts didn't get through. Television is about pushing to the limits, exploring and pushing the envelope further and further. I feel in this department we didn't do that. That we stopped. We didn't experiment more. We didn't push the limits enough. (Producer)

From the perspective of independents struggling on the outside, in-house producers may appear to lead a relatively charmed existence; from the perspective of in-house producers, however, independents are apparently perceived as leading creatively autonomous careers, unfettered by management structures or a conservative programme

78

culture. To what extent the in-house producers' perception of independent production is valid will be examined in detail in Part Two. What is clear is that, as far as the BBC producers are concerned, their own professional and creative energies are squandered by a corporate culture and hierarchy unwilling to innovate, experiment and give full support to producers capable of making new, sometimes challenging, programmes designed to push the conventional boundaries both in terms of form and subject matter:

> I think the hardest thing within the BBC is making a programme that you want to make. If the BBC want to make a programme, you make it from A to Z, and you follow all the procedures all the way down. Whereas, in an independent, they're very open and very aware of taking a chance. They're not afraid to make mistakes, whereas the BBC is very aware of making mistakes. The generals don't like to make mistakes, and that's the plus of independents. They make great programmes, the independents, because they've taken chances. (Researcher)

> Working for the Corporation, I've got a lot of respect for independent programme makers. I am a strong believer in what they make programmes about, letting the programme breathe. They strongly believe in that, whereas the BBC are very tight. They hold on to the programmes all the time. It's extremely difficult to make a programme the way you want to make them. (Researcher)

An Executive Producer lends weight to this researcher's observation in a final statement about the depressive effect of BBC conservatism upon programme ideas:

> The BBC has become so desperate to please that it's forgotten that you can't actually please everyone all the

time. What you can do though is be robust about what you do and defend it. It's almost like they've forgotten how to do that. The major thing really is that air of defensiveness which creates conservatism which means when people jump up and down and they're excited about an idea that sounds a bit iffy, a damp sponge is applied, and they're told to calm down. That robs people of a lot of enthusiasm and again it's quite a demoralising atmosphere to work in. (Executive Producer)

Clearly, the dependence of BBC producers upon senior producers and managers suggests that their position may not be so different from that of many independents. With the BBC increasingly exposed to, and expected to engage with, national and international market forces and broadcasting competition, what gap may once have existed between producers working within an institution committed to public-service ideals and those commissioning programmes on purely commercial grounds in the marketplace of independent television may now have been eroded considerably. A BBC in-house Producer/Director makes exactly this point, and once again indicates how all programme makers, whether BBC in-house or independents, increasingly are forced to anticipate and respond to the Controller's preferred programme requirements:

You're trying to find all the best ways of getting the commission, because it's become a market orientated programme-making style; we no longer have a set budget to make whatever we want. It's no longer like that. It's like, what do we bid for? It's like an auction where the Controller decides what he or she wants: A, B, C and D. And if you've given them all E's you can forget it. So, all in all, I'm afraid that's what we call a market economy. (Producer/Director)

Interestingly, in-house producers are also able to throw some light on

80

the general complaint raised later by all the independents interviewed, namely, the problem of so-called 'sweetheart deals' or the commissioning by senior producers of former colleagues who have set up in business as independent producers and production companies. When discussing the differences between independent and in-house productions, one BBC producer offers insights which help explain the widespread use of 'sweetheart deals' in relation to the commissioning of minority ethnic programme productions:

> It goes back again to the idea of continuity, the ability to bring up trained staff, staff development and so on. The links one can build up from within that as well. The fact is that there are people who work here who are known to people and so I'm not sure, if I was an independent, whether I would have that kind of access to that knowledge and understanding with the community. In technical terms, of course, there is no reason why an independent can't make something as well as we can. If one looks at 'East', I think to be fair almost half of those programmes were actually done by independents anyway. I think our programmes that we made in-house were better but that's biased partly. But, it's not as if it's impossible to do it or anything like that. But, interestingly, those people working in the independents actually had close links with the department in the past and maybe came through the department as well. Um, not that that was because they got the commissions, but because I think they, umm, they had that experience of working within a body of Asian programming. (Producer)

The producer thus points to a number of factors that may contribute to the use of independents known to the producers, as opposed to those who are not. The first, as we can see, relates to the importance attached to the idea of continuity and on-going links with the community. This helps overcome problems of evident community mistrust.

Few producers outside of the department itself are thought likely to have this necessary depth of background experience and involvement. Second, this leads to the likely preferring of former in-house producers because it is precisely they who have managed to accrue this experience and sustain contacts over a considerable time period. They have, in other words, the contacts and the experience in an industry in which such experience is said to be in short supply. However, while experience of working within a body of Asian programming may well be confined, for the most part, to those programme units and departments specialising in such programme making, it seems reasonable to assume that networks and past colleague relationships will also oil the wheels of the commissioning process, a fact that may account for the producer's loss of normal fluency at this point in his statement. When asked to recall some of the independent producers commissioned to work for the Multicultural Programmes Department, it is revealing that all those named by the producer are major independent production companies, none of which, as far as I know, can be considered specialists in Asian programming:

> I'm just trying to think um. From people I know that I have worked with in the past. I know we commissioned something from 'Kilroy Midlands' when he was just starting. From what I can recall on the whole, it seems to be more of a question that freelance producers have come and worked for the department for a period and then left, but in terms of actual independent producers, um, smaller independents, um, I can think of the big ones like 'Diverse' and 'Roger Bolton' and so on, but I can't really say about the small ones. (Producer)

At the very least, it would appear that independents have a distinct advantage if they are either 'known' or 'big', or perhaps ideally both. As we heard earlier, the Multicultural Programme Department has publicly stated how it has 'commissioned several major series from *top* Independent companies' (Morar, 1995, p.7). An in-house producer perhaps sums up the situation as it really is when he states:

> In the case of independents particularly you find that
> it's a very incestuous relationship between the inde-
> pendents and the commissioning bodies. You find that
> everyone knows each other, everyone works on each
> other's programmes, everyone graduated from the
> same class or came from the same place. There is very
> little for new independents, supposing some talented
> Asian programme makers wanted to get their pro-
> grammes commissioned or to do something with good
> ideas. You'd find that it probably wouldn't happen
> and you'd get the same old people making watered
> down versions of them. (Producer)

Finally, it is also instructive to take the opportunity and inquire into a
further complaint voiced later by all the independents about the
commissioning process: its London bias. As will be discussed later,
all the independents interviewed outside of London complain about
the bias towards the capital and the commissioning of major independent companies based there. Again, in-house producers offer some
insight into the nature of the problem. Inadvertently, perhaps, a senior
Executive Producer indicates that there may indeed be a bias against
non-London independent companies in so far as London is thought to
be the only centre for producer talent and also the place where the
majority of the Afro-Caribbean population lives:

> The majority of the Afro-Caribbean population lives in
> London. It's very difficult to convince producers to
> come all the way up to Birmingham to make pro-
> grammes, especially as most of them are good enough
> not to have to leave London to make a programme and
> funds as well.... You're not getting good programme
> ideas from the type of people who should be in the
> department because they're not here.... All my commu-
> nication with audiences, or potential audiences and

programme makers, are at my own instigation and that
invariably means it's only really when I'm in London.
(Executive Producer)

Of course, the demographic and statistical evidence indicates that
London does indeed have a sizeable African-Caribbean community,
but then so too do many other urban centres throughout Britain,
Birmingham and Manchester included. The independents interviewed
for this research indicate that not all of Britain's minority ethnic
producers are confined to London. The established networks of
producer contacts, however, serve not only to advantage and privilege
'known' contacts in relation to London; they also of course disadvantage those who are based elsewhere. This may come as no surprise to
those independent producers based in Bristol and Leeds who were
interviewed for the purposes of this research, but it is clearly a finding
that needs remedying. Britain's ethnic minority communities and
interests cannot necessarily be assumed to be coincident with those in
the capital; ethnic identities and interests are likely to exhibit regional
differences of experience and outlook. These too deserve television
representation.

Summary

Minority ethnic programme makers working within the BBC do not
escape the vagaries of the commissioning process, they, like the
independents, are dependent upon senior commissioners who act as
gatekeepers. Moreover, they work within an institutional environment
which is experienced as relatively exclusive. The majority of producers, and certainly middle and senior management, are said to be white,
middle-class men. The conservative ethos which informs programme
commissioning and production is further traced to the 'Byzantine
bureaucracy' of the BBC - hierarchical, staid and in many respects
non-communicative. Certainly producers find little support from
senior managers to introduce new programme ideas and forms; rather,
the fear of controversy and public criticism tends, if anything, to

squash producer enthusiasm and programme innovation. Interestingly, it was observed how in-house producers tended to view, from their inhibited institutional vantage point, the creative energies of independents as relatively unfettered. To what extent this view matches, in practice, the experience of the independents will shortly be pursued in Part Two of this study. BBC in-house producers have been found to be critically dependent upon senior managers and controllers and obliged to fathom their programme requirements, a task made particularly difficult given the expressed lack of communication and dialogue between senior decision-makers and producers. Moreover, in so far as the BBC has become increasingly exposed to competitive pressures and is organised along the lines of an internal market, so producers also offer up their programme ideas to be bought, or not, according to the 'buying strategy' of senior corporate decision-makers. In all these respects, the professional practices of BBC producers may be found to be not so different from those of the independents working 'outside' in the competitive marketplace.

Commentary by in-house producers on the use of independents also provided an insider's view on so-called 'sweetheart deals' and has revealed something of the professional rationale for this practice, at least in relation to the commissioning of independents to produce minority ethnic programmes. Clearly, the old maxim may still apply - 'It's not what you know, but who you know' that counts. The known commissioning bias towards London's independents has also found some evidential confirmation in the views of a senior executive producer - views that, if enacted, would surely disadvantage producers and African-Caribbean communities located in major urban centres throughout the rest of Britain.

6   Changing times

This last chapter briefly explores the views and concerns of BBC in-house producers about the future of minority ethnic programmes. Their views, perhaps not surprisingly, tend to be closely related to the changing institutional context in which they work, a context which has once again been subject to a radical upheaval with the announcement in September 1995 of the formal dissolution of the Multicultural Programmes Department. This chapter first considers the producers' general views on the future of special multicultural programming provision, before moving on to consider specific responses to the dissolution of the BBC's Multicultural Programme Department and its reconstitution as the Asian Programmes Department, and the more loose arrangement for African-Caribbean programmes. On both counts, the producers' views provide further insight into their understanding of, and rationale for, special programme provision. Generally the producers' views on the future of special multicultural programming production in the BBC tend to be pessimistic. Pervading the producers' comments is a sense that changes in the nature of broadcasting, both internal and external to the BBC, will increasingly erode support for continuing special provision programmes:

I can see in the cold harsh light of reality and the way

television is going, and the way the industry is going, that it will happen. I think it will be a sad day when this department closes, which I think will happen. Not now but in the future, and it will be a sad day. (Producer)

The producer continues, outlining even how the anticipated closure will be justified as well as the continuing relevance, as far as he is concerned, of special multicultural programmes:

I think this department will cease to exist because it's deemed there is no need for it to exist because Asians are completely part and parcel of British life. That would be the excuse used, that you don't need to have separate programmes and you will be served through the existing broadcasting network. That is, via independents or other departments such as news, current affairs, science and features, music, arts, documentary features. They will all have a hand in producing programmes which have an Asian slant or have an Asian content. I feel it will be very sad because we'll lose something like 'Network East' and we have this pool of experience, talented people who know what they are talking about, who know the community inside out. (Producer)

It is expected, then, in the not too distant future, that the BBC will argue that mainstream programmes incorporate minority community agendas and viewpoints and therefore the special departments and programmes can be discontinued. Such a development would not, however, compensate for the loss of certain programmes nor sustain in-depth specialist knowledge and expertise located within specialised departments. The felt need for such departments will inform the anticipated struggle ahead:

We're going to have a difficult job persuading the

87

powers that be that there is a need for the Asian community and the black community to have their own programmes. Multiculturalism is a big umbrella and in an ideal world it would be great if you saw Asians and blacks on mainstream TV all the time without them having to explain why they're Asian or black and they just happen to be there. Sadly, that doesn't seem to be happening and until that happens, until something serious is done about it, then there will always be a need for programmes to be made from the community, for the community. (Researcher)

Moreover, the repercussions of the discontinuation of special programme departments are thought to extend beyond the immediate programmes lost, and affect the available pool of talent capable of making high-quality, knowledgeable programmes across the TV industry as a whole:

I guess it's the old question about the independent system as to whether it really does provide the kind of training and development that a large organisation like the BBC can theoretically do. Now, if the BBC is going to make its own output more independent oriented as well, again is that going to reflect badly on the development of new talent from within the community? You know, the next generation of programme makers. So I think providing the mainstream sources for developing talent should continue because independent producers might find themselves trying to find decent researchers, decent staff or whatever, looking around and finding that those people have not really been brought up to the same kind of standard. (Producer)

Again we hear of the vital training function that such departments, and the BBC more generally, perform and how this will be under threat with the closure of special programme departments. Issues of minority access and opportunity as much as programme representations are relevant considerations here. If the future of special multicultural programming is thought to have a limited life expectancy, the recent dissolution of the Multicultural Programmes Department simply underlines the uncertainties ahead. That said, there had existed for some time a perceived imbalance within the department between Asian and African-Caribbean programme production and output:

> I think that the Afro-Caribbean output was not being served very well at all. The output in terms of the Asian output was being quite well served. It could have been much more progressive; it could have been much more experimental, much more daring. But Afro-Caribbeans I feel just got a completely wrong and raw deal. They need a separate department which will fully document black experience and how black culture is important to everyone, and to themselves primarily. (Producer)

A senior producer also maintained that Multicultural Programme Department failed to provide the 'balance of diversity' within African-Caribbean programmes, leading to critical reactions to some of the department's output:

> We need to make diverse programmes. If we make ten programmes on the Afro-Caribbean community and they're all negative, of course the community is going to be angry about it. If you're not balancing it with some arts or entertainment programmes or programmes like 'Network East'. And that's why I feel there is some conflict, where the Afro-Caribbean community has lost out, because there's not enough diverse programmes made about the community. In the last series of 'All Black', people felt out of ten, eight or nine programmes were really negative: drug use, pros-

titutes, gun runners, and that didn't make a good
impression. Now on 'East' we do the same. It's kind of
looking at the negative side of the Asian community.
But people don't criticise us as much because they feel,
'Oh, we have "Network East", we've got
"Hollywood"', and everything balances out. That's the
major problem, what I would call the balance of diversity. We have to make sure that carries on. The balance
of diversity also leads to the balance of staff. It should
be one of our major functions, training Asian and
African-Caribbean talent. It shouldn't be just our department, it should be the role of the whole community. But because this is a specialist department, you
would expect more Asians or Afro-Caribbeans to
come and do work here, and then move on. (Producer/
Director)

Once again, we hear how community expectations are thought not to
have been met by the limited volume and diversity of output. In
consequence, criticisms of programmes perceived to be 'negative' are
thought to have been all the more vociferous. The opportunities for
training of African-Caribbean recruits, keen to work on
African-Caribbean programmes, were thus also affected adversely.
Programme makers also made reference to the artificial and perhaps
'insulting' nature of having Asian and African-Caribbean programme
making together in the same department. One producer interprets the
department's dissolution thus:

I know the BBC was very concerned about delivering
its Afro-Caribbean output and I think there was a
perception within the industry that it had to get its act
together on it. I think there was some unfair hostility
expressed towards a current affairs series we did called
'All Black' which I wasn't involved in. I think it went
back to the old question of, if you do things that tackle
tough issues, that maybe don't show a community in a

90

wonderful light, then that can provoke something of a backlash. A slightly insulting concept, too, maybe is the idea that very different ethnic groups with different ideas and so on have to be lumped together in a single department, and inevitably that also raises certain political questions as to who is effectively in charge? How do we ensure both areas work? (Producer)

Clearly, as far as the producers are concerned, an imbalance between Asian and African-Caribbean programmes had emerged; a particular and it has to be said highly controversial series of 'All Black' had provoked widespread criticism from the African-Caribbean community - criticism the BBC would rather not have received. The artificial 'lumping together' of different community programmes within the same department had also seemingly caused potential confusion over leadership. Interestingly, two senior BBC managers, both in the same BBC press release, put slightly different glosses on the announced changes:

> We need to give fresh impetus to our programming for African-Caribbean audiences, and to build on the range of our Asian programmes that have a successful 30-year track record. Separating the focal points of African-Caribbean and Asian programme production will enable us to redouble our efforts to meet our ambitions and the expectations of the communities. (Michael Jackson, Controller BBC 2)

> This approach is a logical development for BBC Television's work for both communities. By drawing on all BBC departments and a wide range of independent producers, and supported by the Controller's commissioning and scheduling priorities, African-Caribbean programme output will, I hope, develop well.

Meanwhile I expect to see Asian programming at Pebble Mill go from strength to strength. (Rod Natkiel, Head of Network Television - BBC press release: September 1995c)

A senior producer in the department, though recognising the imbalance in the department between Asian and African-Caribbean programmes, was nonetheless highly critical of the planned change. In fact both the nature of the announcement and the lack of consultation preceding it, simply confirmed her views of the BBC as a bureaucratically remote institution insensitive to the needs of the black community, audiences *and* programme makers - a view elaborated in earlier chapters:

> Audiences are just shocked every time they see something for them on the BBC because it's not habitual enough for them to take it for granted or even assume it's their right. They know it's their right, but they don't assume for that reason it's going to be on air and that's why the last straw, in this kind of cynicism, has been the dismantling of the Multicultural Programme Department and the denial of an Afro-Caribbean Department. The phone calls I'm getting are, 'Well, if there's an Asian Programme Department, why isn't there an Afro-Caribbean Programmes Department?' To which I say, 'I can honestly say, I really, really don't know'. I really don't know. I don't know how you justify that and I wouldn't seek to. Why is there going to be an Executive Producer for Afro-Caribbean programming in Manchester? Why Manchester? No Idea. Don't understand it. Wasn't involved. Wasn't asked. Wasn't consulted. So can't comment and I suppose that's the ultimate feeling. People feel, I mean from the audience right up to programme makers, there is always this awful feeling that people don't trust you.

There's always this feeling that they check you three times rather than once.... I think it's iniquitous to set up a system whereby Asian programming can have an intellectual focus in the Department and Afro-Caribbean programming can't. (Executive Producer)

Clearly, this particular producer feels aggrieved by her lack of involvement and consultation in decisions that will impact upon her personally as well as on the department and the future of African-Caribbean programmes. She acknowledges nonetheless that 'there is at least a public commitment to African-Caribbean programmes in a way that there hasn't been for years'. Uncomfortable facts remain, however: an Asian Programme Department now exists, whereas an Afro-Caribbean department does not; a team of in-house dedicated Asian specialists will continue to produce established and new programmes for principally Asian audiences, whereas Afro-Caribbean programmes will be commissioned on a more piecemeal basis from across mainstream BBC departments and independents by an Executive Producer, not a Managing Editor. Moreover, and perhaps most tellingly, African-Caribbean programming will be 'supported by the Controller's commissioning and scheduling priorities'. These can exert a profound shaping effect on the nature of the programmes eventually commissioned, produced and broadcast.

To what extent BBC 'commissioning and scheduling priorities' can, in fact, give expression to the disparate interests, agendas of concern and programme needs of Britain's black communities can only be known through time. However BBC structures now set in place, and overseen by senior BBC managers, may deliver less than the hoped-for improvements. The reasons for this have been identified throughout the preceding discussion and are summarised below.

Summary

This last chapter of Part One has briefly attended to the views and concerns of in-house BBC producers concerning the future. As far as they are concerned, notwithstanding the evident need for, and benefits of, special minority ethnic programmes and departments, the future looks bleak. This relates principally to the changing nature of broadcasting and the institutional position occupied by the BBC. It is thought likely that special minority ethnic programme departments will be totally closed on the pretext that mainstream departments, across the board, will give adequate expression to minority agendas, values and interests. The producers remain sceptical as to whether mainstream departments can rise to this challenge in the foreseeable future, and point to the impact that such a development would have upon training opportunities and the available pool of expertise and skilled producers working in the television industry as a whole. The most recent decision to split the Multicultural Programmes Department partly confirms their expressed concerns. Recognising the imbalance of programme production and output within the department between Asian and African-Caribbean programmes, producers nonetheless pointed to the apparent unfairness of the latest development which has effectively dispersed African-Caribbean programmes across mainstream BBC departments and independents. A senior producer argued that both the nature of the decision and its bureaucratic implementation, with no consultation, simply confirmed her view of the BBC as an institution insensitive to *both* black audiences and programme makers.

Some of the factors identified throughout the preceding discussion and here thought likely to militate against improved African-Caribbean programmes (notwithstanding the claims made by senior BBC personnel in recent press releases and publicity statements) include the following: the essentially conservative nature and ethos of the BBC, constraining programme subject matter and innovation of programme forms; departmental and producer reluctance to risk public controversy, and thus the tendency to run scared of 'hot' or difficult issues; the professional producers' pursuit of 'mainstream' programmes, audiences and status, and their consequent tendency to water down and 'balance' black perspectives while 'explaining' minority concerns and issues for the benefit of a white audience; the commissioning of programmes from established 'mainstream' production companies, which may not necessarily have the specialist expertise or commitment which are available in less well-established independents; the conventional nature of extant programme forms which may preclude the use of more experimental and dialogical formats; and, not least, commissioning and scheduling priorities, which may well turn out to be increasingly market driven in so far as the competitive pursuit of audience ratings influences the institutional behaviour and programme output of the BBC. These factors, drawn from the preceding chapter discussions, are suggestive only and do not necessarily predict the future of BBC African-Caribbean programmes. They remain, nonetheless, probable shaping forces which together may yet undermine public declarations about the BBC's commitment to improved BBC African-Caribbean programmes.

Asian programming appears to have fared better in terms of BBC institutional commitments and organisational arrangements. A long history of Asian programme production is testimony to this on-going support. Even here, however, concerns and criticisms have been raised by the producers in so far as the factors referred to above also impact on the production of Asian programmes. To these could be added the problem of responding to an Asian population richly differentiated by religion, language, tradition, culture and generation and various geographical and political affinities, as well as differences of class and socio-economic position. Given the producers' pursuit of 'mainstream' programme status, as well as the changing institutional position of the BBC, competing for large audiences within an increasingly competitive environment, the question has been raised whether the BBC will be able to extend its commitments in the future and produce ethnic minority programmes targeted at those communities and sub-groups currently under-represented. Again, when viewed from the vantage point provided by the producers quoted above, the winds of change do not look propitious.

95

Part Two
On the Outside
Looking In:
Independent Producers

I would just like to make a programme that isn't like 'Here we have a minority programme'... I suppose I'm fed up with doing missionary work. (Independent Producer)

7 Aims, access and accountability

An obvious, but nonetheless useful, place to begin this study of independent producers is with the declared aims of the producers themselves (1). Why did they form, or join, independent production companies in the first place and what do they see as the principal aims of their various organisations? Criticisms of television, its representations and production practices are often bound up with underlying views on the 'proper' role and aims of independent producers and their productions. Here an evident difference is found between those relatively well-established and successful independent producers working on major commissions for the BBC and other broadcasting institutions, and those more recently formed, relatively inexperienced and 'community based' independent companies. Two experienced independent producers, both of whom had previously worked successfully for the BBC over a considerable number of years, describe how they progressed 'naturally' from working for the BBC to becoming independents:

> I left the BBC because I found it very limited, very restricted. I am sure lots of things have changed since then, so I am not making any comment about how it is now because it would be inaccurate. But it was a

feeling that I wanted to do drama and branch out. I had worked in the BBC for a long time. (Producer/Director)

When I left high school, I trained in theatre in Toronto, Canada and after that I worked in Paris teaching, but decided I wanted to work in films as opposed to work in the theatre. I got a job at the BBC initially as a researcher in Birmingham and then I got a job in radio drama and finally in television drama, which is what I always wanted to do. I admired the BBC because I went to school in Trinidad, and then I trained. ... I started working with black writers, African, Caribbean, Asian writers, when I was in radio drama. I began developing a database and relationships. When I came to television I continued that work. ... I have two things that I do - I work here as a television drama producer. Obviously the things I do here are fully funded by the BBC. Black Screen is fully funded by the BBC ... I also have an independent production company and we've done various projects which have been funded differently. (Producer/Director)

When asked about basic organisational aims, both producers responded in the terms of the professional producer, preoccupied with the immediate company goals of securing and producing programme commissions:

My company - which for the first time is mine and not a partnership - is called Indigo Productions. It's very much about creating good dramas, very much about creating strong, black feature films, and those are the large projects that I have on board. (Producer/Director)

We have to come up with mainstream ideas that reflect our reality and it isn't being done at the moment. That is why I say it is quite a serious thing - I mean nobody is giving us pocket money to make ghetto programmes any more, and anyway I don't want that. The only thing you can do is compete with the mainstream and it's difficult to know what is going to happen. (Producer/Director)

These established producers, perhaps understandably, have developed a pragmatic stance to their professional position as independent producers. A sense of professional realism, knowing 'realistically' what is possible and what is not in the changing climate of broadcasting, informs their thinking and outlook. They are producers making programmes for the 'mainstream', focused on managing the system as best they can in order to survive commercially, while minimising the extent to which creative programme ideas are compromised. Through force of circumstance, their professional focus tends to be inwards to the survival needs and commercial goals of the independent company itself.

This contrasts with the more outward looking and collectivist ideals informing less well-established, 'community based' independents. Here the question of aims is typically interpreted in much broader, more expressly political, ways:

The argument was that, basically, in this region there is not a film or video organisation to deal with black or ethnic minority groups at all. People go on and on about the under representation of black and Asian people within the industry and that nobody is doing anything about it. At the end of the day, what are they doing about it? We felt what we needed to do was to find the mechanism to give people, first of all, the basic knowledge and then give people the aspiration. Which I think is the biggest problem that we have encountered in bringing black people into the media industry, it is that feeling of non-participation. I mean, I think people really don't feel they have got anything at all to offer, no hope of getting any kind of success in it. (Director/Producer)

For the black community there isn't another organisation like ours within the South West region. I know people keep saying that, but that's the unique position that we hold and, if that's lost, what's the way forward? It's difficult for black people to break into the larger organisations like the BBC, like ITV. If we're given the opportunity to develop ideas here and get them shown on the small screen or in the Arts cinemas, then I think that's a way forward. The initial reason why this project came about was through training and I know we are still committed to giving people the opportunity to train, learning about the business, about the industry. (Co-ordinator)

Here wider concerns of audio-visual black representation are highlighted as a major impetus for the formation of this particular organisation - an impetus which is felt all the more urgently given that it is the only organisation of its kind in the South West region - notwithstanding the fact that both Harlech Television (HTV) and regional BBC are located within the same city. The perceived need for a 'mechanism' to bridge the gap between the black community and the television industry is also clearly stated, with training and motivation identified as critical to the strategy to effect change. A concern with access therefore extends beyond the pursuit of improved programme representations to increased access to the world of television training and programme production. The feeling of 'non-participation' mentioned apparently refers to both the television industry's apparent indifference to black audiences as well as the consequent lack of confidence that this has engendered within the black community itself. Clearly, this organisation has both a mission to improve black access and television representation and a strategy involving practical training and the development of grass-roots television aspirations. Other independents argue similarly:

> Our broad aims are to raise people's confidence who we involve in making these programmes with us and to develop skills, media skills, and also to get people to question, not to accept, the white media that comes in at every pore, and try to empower people. (Artistic Director)

> My aims in this company are to reach out to minorities, to help minority groups to see themselves as important, to give them some form of self-esteem and self-worth, to help them fit in within society, and make positive role models. In the long run it is mainly to develop self-esteem and self-worth in these minority groups. (Producer)

A recurring stated aim across these and other independent production companies, then, is to enhance the confidence of minority ethnic individuals *and* communities in order to increase access to, and active participation in, media production, a view that for some appears to be informed by the notion that the problem is one of lack of self-esteem or self-worth. This view, in turn, supports what may be considered an inflated estimation of the value and effects of positive images. While questions of access and a critical stance towards the range and repertoire of black representations on television inform all the organisations consulted, some appear to have an exaggerated faith in the power of 'positive' images and 'role models' to bring about increased community television involvement and other behavioural changes - a position that we shall see has not gone uncontested. An example of just such a claim, based on this faith in the power of positive imagery, is the following:

> Our aims are to treat these black kids, young people,

with the understanding that they themselves are con-
tributors to society and if they continue on the right
path they have talent, they have good within themselves and they only need to understand themselves to
show it, and to show other people within society.
Another aim is to help them be more honest, more
truthful, to give them hope, to show them that they
are not all thieves and drug pushers and liars and
persons who would steal cars, or the aggressors, the
oppressors, the inferiors - no, they are somebody, a
person. They do have good. We are trying to get this
in front of their faces, so they can actually look and
see themselves that they are good persons and portray
that. ... In any group we have the good and the bad,
and everyone can be good if they want to, and if we
just show them the way, I think they will follow.
(Producer)

While many would probably agree that the television media,
particularly in relation to certain programmes strands and genres, has
produced a surfeit of problem-oriented portrayals of black youth and
thus argue for more diversified characterisations across the spectrum
of programming, this is a far cry from assuming that television
images can be used to socially engineer 'good' behaviour -
assuming, of course, that such is called for. There is no doubting,
however, the commitment that many of the independents interviewed have towards a sense of surrounding community and a desire
to be seen in some respect as pursuing the interests of their
immediate locality:

We can give them hope and give them what they want
to see, being that we are a local company. We are
within them, we are within their community. They
can always pass by, pop in, ask somebody a question.
We are hand to hand with them, face to face, and they
see somebody. If you go to the BBC, they have to go

through so many channels and see that man, and that man and the next one. (Producer)

We are from within the community and we're based locally and, over the past two years, we've established intimate contacts within the community, with various community organisations all round really. I think that gives a kind of intimacy or personal intimate contact with those people and, if we need to tackle any issue, we have built our own personal contacts and we can usually utilise those to be able to make programmes which are of interest. ... Sometimes when black people are represented or portrayed in the media, it's done in a patronising way and, although maybe sometimes they do try to be positive, it comes across as skewed or patronising. But I feel as though it's important for the likes of us, as a minority ethnic production company, to take it in our hands to represent ourselves as befits our community, you know, the people we've been involved with. (Producer)

The sense of an organic connection with local communities, a sense of being part of the same community and responsive to shared problems, is perhaps easier to sustain by newly formed and relatively small-scale production companies than established companies producing programmes aimed at national television audiences. To what extent even locally based companies can be said to be truly 'representative' of these same communities is of course open to question. The notion of 'community' has long proved notoriously difficult to define and pin down, much less research. Even communities of interest are rarely bounded simply by locality or informed solely by face-to-face relationships. Moreover, on closer inspection identified 'communities' tend to reveal a range of differences, and sometimes deep schisms, of interest and outlook; differences that render problematic assumed notions of a common existence, shared interests *and* the pursuit of faithful 'representation'. While claims can readily be made of 'representing the community', these organisations are not in any practical or meaningful way accountable to them. This is not to deny their evident genuineness of commitment, nor possible feelings of moral solidarity and responsibility. It is to suggest, however, that to speak in the name of 'the community' demands some critical reflection on the 'representativeness' of the organisation, its aims *and* its accountability.

A more tangible measure of involving members of minority ethnic communities within the aims and activities of the different companies can be seen in relation to the provision of training, a stated aim of all the 'community-based' independents interviewed. This widespread desire to help others gain a foothold on the ladder of television production demonstrates the collectivist ideals informing these organisations:

> I think sometimes when we talk about black programming, the major concentration is on directors and producers and the editorial side of programming. But I do think that much more important than that is the development of skilled personnel. And a decent production staff pool within the North is vitally important in terms of the work of the organisation. I think we have spent a lot of time trying to build that infrastructure from the bottom up, because I think it's not good enough just to complain about the exclusion of black talent from the production market. I think it is important to do something about it and I think it's a source of great pride to our organisation that we are actually willing to address that on a small measure, given that we have limited resources, given that we are a young organisation. (Training Co-ordinator)

> We have our own ideas about what we feel is needed to actually bring people through, and I think the most important thing for me is that people get to the stage

where they are actually not just making the projects, but are actually involved in the decision-making in terms of governing the finances. I think that's a crucial element for black organisations and for independent organisations to go forward in that a lot of the time they ain't involved in the money making decisions and they get overlooked by the more established organisations like the broadcasters offering training. ... I think people are sometimes blinded by the romanticism of being a black director. They don't realise that the most important part of it, or one of the most important parts of it, apart from the producer of the project, is putting the deals together. (Co-ordinator)

The pursuit of training may also be seen as a way of building bridges to the major regional television institutions:

I think that's something we will take to them again and sort of court the idea of people doing some placements with them. Maybe that would be a way of us establishing some sort of contact with them on a commercial basis in doing some small commissions with them. (Co-ordinator)

Concerns of training, increased community involvement and television access and programme representation generally inform the organisational aims and ethos of many of the smaller organisations, a line of continuity that stretches back, perhaps, to the black workshop movement of the 1980s.

Summary

From the above discussion of the independents' organisational aims, a number of salient themes and concerns have become apparent. An evident difference of aims was identified between the well-established and more commercially oriented producers and the less established, more 'community-based' independents. Whereas a more pragmatic stance towards programme making and programme ideas produced for the mainstream was apparent in the former, a broader, more outward-looking and collectivist approach informed the latter. Increased television access is typically conceptualised as having a double, though interrelated, aspect for the community-based independents. Increased and enh,anced black representation on screen is thought, in considerable measure, to be dependent upon increased representation in positions of authority and influence behind the screen. The importance of training and opportunities to gain confidence in, and the basic knowledge about, television production has thus become a basic aim declared by all the community- based independents consulted.

Some have gone further, however, and maintained that the problem of access is one of low community and individual self-esteem, in part related to the debilitating nature of television's representations. This position probably gives an inflated estimation to the power of television's images, and inevitably moves towards a politics of representation which seeks to produce 'positive' countering images. This position, as documented in the following chapter, is not uniformly held across the independents consulted however. A further concern relating to the politics of representation has also been raised. This concerns the sometimes problematic claims made by some of the producers to be *in*, *from* or *of* the community and thus 'representative' and able to speak on its behalf. The essentially contested ideas of 'community' and shared interests, however, render problematic self-declared claims to be representative. Also, the silence surrounding the concomitant ideas to 'representation' and 'representativeness' - those of delegation, mandate and accountability - has also been observed and commented upon.

Note

1 The numbers of producers from ethnic minorities currently

working as self-employed independents or as employees of independent production companies are difficult to determine. In part this relates to the highly fluid nature of independent production and organisations, whether commercial and/or community-based. The situation is not monitored by the Producers Alliance for Cinema and Television (PACT), Channel Four nor by any other likely organisation. Though directories of commercial production companies are available and annually up-dated (e.g. Peak, 1995; Peak and Fisher, 1996) listing, currently, over 600 companies, these provide the barest information and do not indicate how many or to what extent they are involved in the production of programmes aimed specifically at ethnic minorities. Producers working in the field and interviewed for this research estimate, however, that only a handful of companies are regularly involved in the production of such programming, though the field of new and aspiring independents working in and around community-based organisations is wider (and more transitory).

8 The cultural politics of representation

A major motivation for setting up and working within independent production companies, as we have heard, is to produce and help others produce 'improved' programmes for minority ethnic communities. Inevitably, such a project gives rise to a host of issues and concerns that together can be addressed as the 'cultural politics of representation'. What, exactly, is being called for and what is the proposed route to, or strategy for, enhanced representation? Here a number of positions can be identified across the producers interviewed. Though there is much common ground, there are also subtle, and sometimes not so subtle, differences of analysis and of advocated approach. Again, the established independents can be contrasted to the newly emergent companies.

An established producer indicates something of her broad approach when decrying the current lack of availability of funds, while nonetheless rejecting what she sees as 'ghetto' funding:

> There is more commercialism in broadcasting now.
> The whole culture of handouts, of 'let's have a little
> black scheme there, and let's give black people a little
> bit of pocket money', are actually going out and
> nobody wants it any more - black people don't want

to do it. I find I don't want to do it, black film makers
don't want to do it.... (Producer/Director)

What others may see as part of a necessary 'enclave strategy', a
deliberate policy to commission and/or produce special programming for ethnic minorities and thus help establish their presence
within the television industry, is here apparently interpreted as a
form of tokenism. In an environment in which funding is acknowledged to be increasingly scarce, professional expediency as much as
a position on the cultural politics of representation probably informs
the producer's outlook. In order to survive in an increasingly market
driven and commercial context, the producer needs to be taken
seriously on grounds of professional talent, not perceived patronage.
Though some producers, as we shall hear later, may also question the
long-term virtues of 'ghetto' programming and funding, most are
less cavalier about saying 'nobody wants it anymore'. Not that this
producer is under any illusion about the virtues of the mainstream:

> I think that if you are working in television now, you
> have to have a mainstream agenda. I don't think
> there is a marginal, a non-mainstream agenda, any
> longer. But the mainstream doesn't do anything for
> images of blackness so if you're involved in this
> business, you have to deal with that. You have to
> deal with the fact that there is no space, all the little
> ghettos are gone. .... There aren't any more black
> programmes being made now than there were ten
> years ago - if anything less. We haven't broken into
> the mainstream. There are more of us producers, at
> the same time there are all these commercial pres-
> sures on the white institutions that make them much
> more selective about what they do, so the pressures
> are different and it still means the black product is
> being excluded from the so-called mainstream. One
> is on the look out to see what are the openings, what

we can do to make our voices heard. (Producer/
Director)

This established producer, then, is critical of the mainstream and its
lack of 'black product', funding and time for minority ethnic representation. In calling for more black voices, she makes reference to
the voices of black producers particularly. In terms of the cultural
politics of representation, a key question to ask here is whether these,
in turn, are thought to be representative of wider perspectives and
positions found within the black community. Is this the role and
responsibility of a black producer?

> All I can do as a black producer, or a black director,
> or a black artist, is do what I think is truthful to my
> experience. The essence of a rich culture will be
> enormous diversity - as much diversity as there are
> individuals to express a vision. (Producer/Director)

Informing this view of black culture is a recognition of individual
diversity, creativity and the need to grant it expression. This is not,
in other words, a view which carries a representative torch for the
black community, or indeed any other wider political position. In the
same interview, the producer went on to discuss a new project
underway, revealing something of the challenges and excitement of
producing for the mainstream:

> It's an adaptation. It's just in the very early stages of
> development at the moment. ... It's quite a commer-
> cial idea, and I find it quite exciting the idea of having
> black men, black women and black children in a kind
> of 'Thirty Something'-relationship drama series, as
> opposed to something about racism. I am very excited
> about that and I think those opportunities to make
> mainstream things, what's nice about it is that, if it's
> done in the right way, I think it could be accessible to
> white women. (Producer/Director)

Once again, the pragmatics of dealing with the mainstream have, in this instance at least, been enthusiastically pursued as a professional challenge. Commercialism and mainstream audiences apparently inform the producer's thinking as much as ideas about positive portrayals and black relationships. Other, less established, independents are less well disposed towards the representational benefits of the mainstream however. Statements from a number of independents, already cited in Chapter Seven, indicated a particular representational aim and associated cultural politics. A further view is the following which not only criticises television's current representations, but also clearly signals a way forward:

> The most important aim that we have is to enlighten people about black issues. That's the most important aim. We want to present a picture of black people which we think is realistic, is truthful, that deals with the kind of problems that black people face in their everyday life. ... There is a lot of white people out there with a lot of prejudices about black people and we want to show them that their prejudices are wrong and that we're just like everybody else, but with our own culture, own community and that we want to express ourselves. We want it to be done accurately and we are sick and tired of all the rubbish that is being put out about black people. So that's what we want to happen. To put across the message that will break down ignorance, to help encourage truth and accuracy, to use everything at our disposal to be effective producers. To get more and more people at grass roots level involved in the media, because a lot of black people are interested, but they don't have the courage and the confidence to come and use all the equipment and learn how to use the media so they can become producers themselves at different levels. (Director)

Here the criticism extends to calls for change; that is, more 'realistic', 'truthful' and 'accurate' pictures. In contrast to the established producer's viewpoints above, in which the cultural politics of representation is confined to calls for increased opportunities for the creative expression of diverse individual 'visions', here the critical benchmark of communal reality and experience is invoked. The difference of approach goes deeper than variations in referenced programme form, whether drama or factual programming. In the established producer's view, cultural politics is relativised and apparently atomised into a diversity of voices; in the case of this community-based producer, cultural politics, in contrast, becomes objectified and solidified. The problem with the latter is not only its challenge to a perceived overly negative and restricted television agenda (a description which may now be less than accurate), but also the way in which 'truth', 'accuracy' and 'realistic' pictures are assumed to be known by the producer and to be beyond dispute. The challenge to television's representations is advanced, in other words, from a position of assumed objectivity, standing above the fray as it were, rather than from the position of an engaged disputant. This is not to suggest that, in matters of detail and basic fairness, such criticisms cannot be made against television and its representations. Simply that when it comes to identifying 'black issues' and their subsequent interpretation and treatment, these are inescapably political and open to contestation. This is so whether calling into play wider social viewpoints or those internal to the so-called 'black community'.

This producer also entertains a strong belief in the educative capacity of the television medium to both enlighten and dispel white prejudices - a view that many may argue is overly optimistic. Again we hear the diagnosis of low access as being due to low confidence, and the consequent organisational aim of encouraging more people to become involved as practitioners. Interestingly, when it comes to ideas about programme design and appeal, outlined by the same director below, there *is* a recognition of the differentiated nature of the 'black community', but this does not follow through into appreciating the implications of this for a more pluralised view of 'realistic' representations. Not all representations may comfortably be accommodated to a 'black perspective'. Indeed, as the notion of the end of 'the essential black subject' suggests, some may even challenge the idea itself (as discussed in Chapter One, and Chapter One, note 1):

> We recognise at New Image that what we have to say
> is not going to address all black people, so we try to
> make the stories as diverse as possible, to appeal to
> different sections of the community. So anybody
> from the older generation to the younger generation,
> to people in between, people from Trinidad, from the
> people of Jamaica who like different things from the
> people from Barbados. We try to hook into what the
> community wants. We know what the community
> wants because we are from the community, and once
> we know, so we understand how important it is. So
> we think that we can contribute diversity and interest
> to hook into the interests of the black communities
> around the country because, once they listen to what
> we have to say about our community, then they will
> be able to relate to it. And it's going to be something
> that they're going to hook into round the country. So
> we want a black centred interest which the media
> don't have; the media don't talk about things from a
> black perspective, which we think we have to offer.
> (Director)

Perhaps a more sophisticated view on the cultural politics of representation is found in the following, in which the problem is recognised to be one of the under-representation of the *diversity* of voices and experiences that are currently available:

> I understand that black programming is there to ad-
> dress issues of representation and I think that is really
> a legacy of the kind of campaigning that was done by

black media workers in the late 70s and early 80s. It is understood generally that what is required in television, particularly within drama, is integrated casting and that would resolve the whole issue of the exclusion and representation of black people. But I think there is another, more important, issue that is allied to the question of voices: *stories*. I think representation is not just about the appearance of black faces and black skins on the TV screens. I think it is crucially about the kind of voices and the kind of stories that must come from the black communities. The kind of stories that speak to the aspirations and expectations of black people. The kind of stories that would contribute to genuine multicultural societies. These types of opportunities I feel are few and narrow and by and large should be available at the level of writing and at the level of creating those stories and telling those stories. It is not just simply about a few black characters in Coronation Street or a Pizza Hut owner in Brookside, or a meandering unemployed hairdresser on one of the other London soaps. (Training Co-ordinator)

This view provides an intermediate position on the cultural politics of representation in relation to those outlined so far. It neither entirely dissolves the idea of black culture into atomised individual voices, each supposedly equally deserving of television expression; nor does it argue in solidified terms for a uniform black perspective buttressing an objectivist view of representation. Rather, it calls for the expression of a plurality of black viewpoints and voices whose stories deserve to be heard; stories that resonate with different histories and experiences within the black communities; stories that cannot be told if the aim is confined to calls for 'equal opportunities' and integrated casting.

As discussed in Part One, the phrase 'the burden of representation' has been used in recent years to describe the particular situation of black producers who feel a responsibility to use every opportunity to challenge dominant media representations and negative portrayals. This makes for extremely crowded and ideologically busy representations, often shaped in terms of the dominant portrayals, albeit now often in inverted ways with deliberately countering representations. An independent explains:

> (The) general exclusion of the 60s and 70s produced a campaigning movement that ultimately resulted in the institutions taking black production seriously. Part of the legacy from that is the attitude among certain sections of the community, by no means the entire community, that black representation should be addressed in a particular way. That is, the production of black images from within the black community is governed by sensitivities in terms of positive role models, in terms of critiquing the stereotypes, or the insistence in depicting certain issues that emerge from the community, and not others. I am referring of course to exposes of the kinds of problems that happen within the black community, whether cultural difficulties, issues of crime, education and under-achievement amongst black children. I think there is a whole host of issues that if we look back. I think ruffled a few sensitivities. (Training Co-ordinator)

Interestingly, not all producers apparently consider community expectations as a 'burden' at all, in the sense of constraining producer autonomy and creativity, but rather as a shared responsibility to produce more serious, positive and accurate community images:

> We have a situation where the few black people that there are on TV, because of all the racism, they get misrepresented on TV. They get problems with the way they show them as drug pushers, pimps, greedy all the time and all the kinds of stereotypes like that.

117

And when you watch the news about black people, all the news reports, they make black people seem like criminals all the time, you know. Always criminals. So I think, as a film and video producer, black people recognise that I've got an important tool in my hand to make a change. And black people know that the kind of shit that they see on TV is not them at all, so they expect me, as a producer, to produce accurate documentary programmes to dispel all the rubbish that is put out about us. ... The expectation is that we produce serious programming about the black community because there is not enough serious black programming on TV. So we carry the weight of the community on our shoulders. Sometimes we fail. There are so many issues that are not addressed that black people want us to look at. We feel we are carrying the weight of it all on our shoulders. (Director)

I think these minority groups expect us to produce films that are documentaries that show the truth about the black people, to give all the people a different side of the story, a true story about themselves, instead of hearing all this thing and being put in the wrong all the time. (Producer)

The weaknesses of this particular position on the cultural politics of representation have been raised already. Other producers, in contrast, have expressed various conflicts and tensions that follow upon their 'privileged' position as producers. One producer describes at length how he experiences the 'burden of representation' and the double-sided complexity involved:

The problem with the burden of representation is that it comes from both sides. You get it from the black community and you get it from out there, from people who are not black. They already have a whole load of preconceptions, preconceptions about who you are and what you're going to say. If you don't say that, then they're going to get very, very nervous because they don't actually know what you're doing and that really worries them. You know, it really, really worries them, especially among white commissioning editors, or the power structures that give money for production to happen. They don't like that. If you tell them, you know, 'I'm going to make a film about boys n'the hood and there's going to be lots of crack, and people are going to get shot, and there's a guy who's trying to better himself and he's trying to go to school'. And they say, 'yeah, yeah, that's alright. Yeah, that sounds great'. You know, you say, 'I want to make this film about some white guys that build ships and it's a really happy story about the working class, and the development of the working class and how they've lost their jobs' (sic). 'Yeah, but you're black, aren't you?' That's what you'll get, without a shadow of a doubt. If, as a black film maker, I want to make a film that has no black subject in it at all, they will look at me and they will defy my capability to do so. (Producer)

This provides an unusual insight into the so-called 'burden of representation', drawing attention to the pressures and expectations placed upon black film makers and programme makers by white commissioners, an aspect explored further when discussing gate-keepers and commissioners in Chapter Ten. The producer next outlines what he experiences as the other side of the burden of representation, as exerted by the black community:

On the other side, in the black community, there is a burden about positive representation. You're not al-lowed to be just a film maker. If somebody feels that, within the film the representations of black people are not good, they will use that to beat you over the head with. With the most amazing brutality really, considering that obviously this is a person, and this is how they see the world and this is what they want to say, et cetera, et cetera. So, much of the work can really run into trouble with the black community even though so much of the work is up-front politically, up-front about challenging these assumptions within the narrative structures, within the visual language. People, black communities, say 'What's this? This is crap'. And, 'He's gay and he shouldn't really be. What is that saying about black people?' You know, all this kind of stuff. It is an almost unbearable burden because you're just not allowed to speak without that context on both sides. It's that burden they put on you to represent positively and you can't do it like that, I don't think. You have to tell the story as the story is. If I was going to make a film... I wouldn't be able to guarantee that all the representations you would get in there of black people would be positive, and I wouldn't want to. Because I think it is as important to discuss the good things within our community as it is to discuss the things that are problematic. And that's important and a sign of maturity within our community. (Producer)

Here we have a clear indication of the sorts of pressures, the sorts of expectations, that are felt to be placed upon the black producer by the wider black community, a finding confirmed in part in a further research study (Halloran, Bhatt and Gray 1995, pp.20-29).

That study references a number of criticisms made by minority ethnic audiences of special and general minority ethnic programme provision, including the very same sorts of criticisms recounted by the producer above. It is also interesting to note that the basis of community complaints appears to be both about programme content *and* programme form. Reference to 'challenging assumptions' within the 'narrative structures' and 'visual language' of television, points to the attempted development of a different television aesthetic or regime of programme representation. Evidently audience expectations on occasion may well lag behind the creative intentions of programme makers in matters of form as much as political content. With regard to the audience's expectations of programme makers to produce 'positive' images - a position seemingly shared by at least some independent producers - the producer goes deeper and provides an analysis for this:

> This thing about positive representation, I think half of it is not the black community looking in. It's not an internal thing. It's us looking out and saying we've got to convince them that we're better than they think we are. I think that is a really bad battle to fight, because I don't think you're going to win that one. They'll see you how they want to see you. ... If they see the representations, people will begin to understand black people are not as homogeneous and narrow and easy to define as they perhaps thought. That's what I believe the way forward is. It's to approach it like that.
> But it really is an intolerable burden I have to say, and one that winds me up no end really. (Producer)

Audience expectations and criticisms are thus related to the wider social conditions and changing politics of 'race', the seemingly inescapable context of black film and programme making. It is perhaps unsurprising, given the limits exerted by such a context, that programme makers may on occasion seek to shake off their burden of representation:

> I would just like to make a programme that isn't like 'Here we have a minority programme'... I suppose I'm fed up with doing missionary work. (Producer)

Summary

This discussion has gone a little deeper into the underlying aims of independent producers outlined in Chapter Seven. Attending to the cultural politics of representation, a number of producers' positions on the deficiencies and problems of television's representations have been discerned, as well as related programme strategies for improvement. Established producers working in the competitive environment of mainstream television have noted the drying up of 'ghetto' funding previously targeted at black producers and programmes, perceiving such funding, in any case, as a form of tokenism. The mainstream, though currently not disposed to support or encourage black programming, is the terrain on which black programme makers must compete and struggle for commissions. An established producer's position on the cultural politics of representation was also outlined, a view apparently informed by a highly individualist understanding of cultural creativity and expression. Community-based and emergent production companies, in contrast, held more collectivist, though internally differentiated, positions on black cultural representation. Differences emerged between those who diagnosed the problems of television representation as ones of inaccuracy, lack of truthfulness and negativity, leading to calls for more accurate, truthful and positive images, and those who, recognising the differentiated nature of the black communit*ies* and inevitable contestation over key issues, called for pluralised access to the multiple voices and experiences currently found within *and* across black communities.

The so-called 'burden of representation' was explored and was found also to be differently interpreted and experienced by a number of producers. Some interpreted the burden in ways sympathetic to the criticisms advanced by some audience members, identifying with calls for more 'serious', 'truthful' and 'accurate' representations. Others pointed to a more complex, more onerous situation relating to felt expectations emanating from *both* white commissioners and black audiences, and relating to considerations of *both* representational content *and* form. As black programme makers producing programmes in a wider, racially stratified, context, for many it appeared difficult to see how the burden of representation could be lifted. Such may be the fate of the politically-engaged programme maker.

9 Controls, constraints and limitations

This chapter and the next outline some of the major controls, constraints and limitations identified by independent production companies in their bid to survive and make the types of programmes that they deem to be necessary. Of course, controls, constraints and limitations have already been addressed in a way in Chapters Seven and Eight, with their discussions of organisational aims and representational politics. Though these may not necessarily be construed negatively by those involved, such normative aims and ideals exert, as we have seen, their own shaping influence upon programme content and form. The organisational goals pursued, and the cultural politics enacted, delimit programme production in particular ways, ways which impact upon considerations of selected subject matter and treatment, and programme form.

The review of positions on the cultural politics of representation also identified the so-called 'burden of representation' as a potential shaper of subject choice and programme treatment. Though few producers are likely to concede to having been directly influenced by audience preferences and perspectives in ways they disagreed with, it is a brave/foolhardy programme maker who ignores his/her potential audience completely. Moreover, the influence of shifting cultural politics does not necessarily work at the level of conscious and instrumental thought alone, but also perhaps more 'atmospherically' as part of the cultural air we breathe. In so far as some producers are situated within particular political/cultural atmospheres sustained both inside and outside of their respective organisations, so they both contribute to, and are sustained by, prevailing political cultural climates.

This chapter, however, is concerned with some of the more immediate practical difficulties and limitations faced by independent producers and their organisations. It examines problems of scale, funding and location, with Chapter Ten pursuing related concerns such as with key contacts with, and dependencies on, institutional decision-makers, commissioners and other gatekeepers. This chapter now turns to the first of the self-identified problems confronting independent producers, the problem of scale and its inter-relationship with the problem of funding.

> It is always difficult for small companies because you tend to be funded on a project-by-project basis and there is the danger that, because the production fee is being squeezed by certain large organisations, you haven't enough money to survive in between times; you are always on the basis of putting all your energies into getting one production going. Then you have that space of, 'right you've finished that', you've then got to look for more money. Where I want to be is to get a slate of productions going, which gives you the cash flow to survive, gives you the ability to take on other people. And so that is a more viable situation. A lot of companies are very tiny, like myself, and that makes it very difficult to survive. (Director/Producer)

In an increasingly competitive market place, stimulated by Government policies of deregulation and, following the 1990 Broadcasting Act, the stipulation on broadcasters to commission at least 25 percent of all productions from independents, this producer has to juggle her time and resources between finding, planning and bidding for new programme commissions at the same time as working on current commissions. Small companies that cannot enjoy the efficiencies of scale or the developed division of labour sustained by larger companies, are at an obvious disadvantage by virtue of their size alone (1). The problem is further compounded, particularly for small companies, by the squeeze on production fees brought about by increased market competition and deregulation. Whereas the bigger companies can aim to stagger production and commission bids in a constant flow, cross-subsidising different projects, such flexibility is denied the small independent. Moreover, without the resource base and increased flexibility of a large company, the small independent is also at a disadvantage when competing for major projects. This relates to structural characteristics of the company itself, and not simply the possible 'sweetheart' relationships enjoyed between particular independents and commissioners (discussed later):

> We are going through a transition phase. It was never going to happen overnight. ... The difficulty is that there are now established, large independents who are known to broadcasters and it is still the case, and I think it is not just a feeling or a prejudice, that they will hear about the larger scale productions for series, or they will have more of an opportunity to do it. This is not a complaint; I am also saying that this is the situation and maybe black independents should be grouping together to take on large-scale projects. (Director/Producer)

This refers to commercial commissions from major television institutions, as described by an established commercial independent. The funding situation for less established independents is, if anything, even more precarious:

> A lot of my time has been spent in actually dealing

126

with funders and trying to push the organisation forward and trying to create some cash flow for the actual project. There is a problem there in that, because we only receive x amount of money to do a full-time job, we receive about a quarter of that, so they are asking us to do the same amount of work for a quarter of the amount they actually give us. (Co-ordinator)

Constantly under-funded, the co-ordinator of this production company argues that no wonder so many people develop a cynical attitude to funders:

A lot of time people say that voluntary organisations are given money to fail. Black voluntary organisations are given money to fail. They're only given a certain amount to do things and, when they fail, they say, 'They couldn't deal with it. You're a typical black organisation and you don't know how to deal with things'. They go to the wall. There's not enough cash to actually go forward and develop a structure for a project. (Co-ordinator)

Funding from grant-awarding bodies is increasingly tight in the 1990s. The vibrant black workshop sector, sustained in part by Channel Four, the British Film Institute, Regional Arts Boards and municipal councils in the 1980s, no longer enjoys such support. Moreover, seeking out funding from grant-awarding agencies and institutions is said to place the receiving organisation in a double bind. If such funding remains insufficient, which is often the case (as indicated above), other sources of finance, including commercial revenue, has to be sought. However, commercial revenue, if secured, can jeopardise continuing support from grant-awarding bodies.

Black Pyramid was receiving monies from the Local

Authority and from the Regional Arts Board (South West Arts). They're restructuring so money is tighter, and Avon's folding (Avon County Council was abolished in May 1996). We received money from Avon, we haven't got a look in from Bristol City Council yet. Should we be so reliant on these organisations to actually keep us going, or should we be more reliant on ourselves in developing projects that can be commissioned, developing ideas and touting our own business instead of being reliant on these people? But then, again, if you start doing that, they look at you and say, 'Oh, these guys are making money on their own, so we've got to cut this umbilical cord that we have with you and you've got to deal with it on your own.' (Co-ordinator)

Different funding strategies are also, of course, intimately related to the types of projects and programmes that can be produced:

I think we have a responsibility to our audience. The trouble is that the major responsibility is to funders. I think we tend to be seen by funders in a very stereotyped way and I think that does produce, it puts us into, it gives us a boundary that we might not have chosen ... but at the end of the day we want money. If you haven't got money, it doesn't matter how great your ideas are, you need money. ...We all have other jobs. The major funding comes in our educational work. It's harder getting funding for the sort of stuff we really want to do ourselves. (Artistic Director)

The struggle for funds proves a constant source of concern and a drain on an organisation's energies. The relatively 'shoe string' condition of many independents is illustrated in the funding strategies of the following:

For funding, for sources of funding, we have to try to obtain money from the local grant agency. We also try to raise money. We have a guy called Mike who runs a music system, who runs a disco, and he is based at our centre. So we pay Mike to organise a music festival for us every so often and we take some of the money and put it into the film company. So he uses our premises and some of our equipment and we get some of that back from the concert. We also get money from the training courses that we run for people, like we have someone who comes in who can run a production training course for us, and the money that people pay to do the course is the money that we use to help to make our films. (Producer)

Funding is obviously fundamental to the success or failure of independent productions. The feeling of most producers is perhaps best summed up as follows:

And you think to yourself, is this going to be the norm for black organisations. Are they going to have constantly to go here, there and borrow money every-where to get their projects made? (Co-ordinator)

A further constraint experienced by many independents, a constraint that also relates to lack of funding opportunities, is location. A constant refrain by all the producers based outside London is that of 'London bias', first raised in Chapter Five when discussing the commissioning of independents from inside the BBC:

I think nothing exists outside of London when it comes to film and video. Really and truly. It's just the way it runs. If you live in London you tend to get more access to funds. London is where it's at. Every-where else is kind of slightly provincial and slightly not really happening. As a black film and video organisation functioning outside of London, we perceived ourselves for a long time, whether this is true or not, because obviously the networks for information are not always as good as they could possibly be, we perceived ourselves as being the only black video workshop outside of London for at least a couple of years. Wherever I went, people automatically assumed I was from London. (Producer)

The complaint of London bias is compounded by the nature of regional programming produced by broadcasting institutions, both ITV and BBC, based within the regions:

The complaint is that there isn't much programming production that comes from the regions. There isn't particularly the kind of regional diversity that for instance you see in other television programme strands, compared to what actually is beamed out in terms of minority ethnic programmes. That's the general situation. So basically in Leeds we don't particularly have opportunities for broadcast, although Leeds is a centre for regional broadcasting because Yorkshire Television is based here. But their output, in terms of minority ethnic programmes, is limited to public action or community action programmes, public information notices and a bit of religious multi-faith spots. In terms of national broadcasting, of course, the opportunities that are opened up both within the BBC and within Channel Four you could assume are also open for regional production companies. But the reality is that most of the output of these national networks is heavily concentrated in London, in terms of production, in terms of the ideas and in terms of the kind of material that is reflected on those channels. (Training Co-ordinator)

The geographical separation from London distances producers from key networks of gatekeepers and commissioners and sources of vital information, despite efforts on the part of the independents and Channel Four to address the situation:

> I don't know if we're missing somebody's mailing list or something like that, but we don't seem to get a lot of the information. That's the thing. You have to go through all these sorts of mazes to actually get to the cash. (Co-ordinator)

> In terms of our dealing with Channel Four, we do look out for all the news releases, whether they are competitions or invitations to submit ideas, new directors. We do look at the trade press in terms of what commissioning editors have openings for and we are actually regularly getting information from Channel Four, information regarding commissioning for new programmes and new programme strands. We also attend workshops held locally or in London by commissioning editors to explain any new changes of policy or any new directions that commissioning editors may be taking in relation to future programming. Now that's pretty standard stuff in terms of the kind of contacts between production companies and Channel Four commissioning editors and offices of assistant commissioning editors. We also organise our own invitations to writers, writer-producers associated with Hall Place studios. That in a sense is our total contact with Channel Four. We do submit ideas unsolicited to commissioning editors and I must say that, overall, one could say that one is pretty satisfied with the level of contacts. But what is quite obscure for anybody who doesn't live in London and is not part of that wider network of producers and commissioning editors and that kind of social scene,

is that you don't tend to get the feel of future trends and future directions that companies may be taking, although reading the trade press may give you clear ideas. But it is always difficult to discern what is coming up through that kind of avenue. So it is a weakness being in the region. (Training Co-ordinator)

Summary

Some of the major constraints and limitations identified by independent producers and their organisations relate to scale, funding and locality. Small-scale organisations are disadvantaged in an increasingly competitive marketplace; they neither have the economic efficiencies or degree of control over the production process that their larger competitors have, nor do they have the latter's capacity for a refined and continuous specialist division of labour. Wearing multiple hats, producers are compelled to perform diverse tasks as best they can during the production of commissions.

A key task, of course, is the constant pursuit of funding. Here a reduction in available funding through grant-awarding bodies and a driving down of commission fees by broadcasting institutions, themselves working within an increasingly competitive environment, are said to have further exacerbated what for many is, organisationally and personally, a 'hand-to-mouth' existence. Both established independents producing for the mainstream and community-based organisations are confronted with the constant problem of securing funds in order to survive. When funding is secured, problems of under-funding increase the possibility of project failure. Attempts to build a patchwork quilt of funding from both grant-awarding institutions and commercial sources have also resulted in a double bind in which grant-awarding institutions are less disposed to support commercially-oriented organisations, notwithstanding their financial need of such support.

Finally, funding problems are compounded by the 'London bias' which serves to marginalise and disadvantage independents based in the regions. Poor communications and distance from important networks (involving key gatekeepers and commissioners based in the capital), notwithstanding institutional and independent efforts to overcome both, further disadvantage independents in the regions. The nature of broadcasting produced/commissioned by major tele vision institutions currently permits little scope for regionally commissioned and produced minority ethnic programmes, a finding pursued further in the following chapter.

Note

1 A recent commentator on the changing nature of Channel Four and its involvement of independents poses fundamental questions concerning the financially precarious situation of small-scale producers seeking commissions from Channel Four: 'While it is true that Channel 4 provides some opportunities for first-time film-makers and for those who would otherwise have no access to television, the problem for the small independents is "how to survive" in the face of radical uncertainty about the renewal of production contracts. As the individuals who make up the sector get older, take on domestic commitments and realize the benefits of secure employment, a predictable income, sick pay, paid holidays and properly resourced pensions, their commitment to working in a radically insecure sector inevitably diminishes. It is appropriate, therefore, to ask whose cultural and economic interests are served by the maintenance of this sector and this "miniature" mode of production? And to what extent are freedom and diversity of expression safeguarded for the television audience by this system of production?' (Harvey, 1994, p. 125). The producers interviewed for this study are likely to recognise the deprivations and temptations described; from their position as aspirant programme-makers seeking commissions in the imperfect world of British television, they are also, perhaps, more inclined to make 'relative' judgements about the virtue

of Channel Four and its role in sustaining independents (see Chapter Ten). This is not to say that fundamental questioning of Channel Four and its involvement in sustaining (precariously) small-scale production companies is not also required in relation to the wider conditions and contexts of independent production.

10 Commissioners, gatekeepers and sweethearts

Independent producers seeking programme commissions are critically dependent upon commissioners and senior corporate decision-makers. These gatekeepers occupy a pivotal role in determining which programme proposals get considered, developed and made, and which do not. They constitute, in other words, a further crucial shaping influence upon the production of minority ethnic programmes. Independent producers are positioned, as we have seen, in relation to organisational aims and contending views on the cultural politics of representation, as well as in an increasingly competitive and stratified marketplace. They also occupy a position of institutional dependence on key gatekeepers. Gatekeepers are themselves, of course, also surrounded by commercial, institutional and cultural forces, and manage their position accordingly; they are perhaps no less subject to systems of constraint and influence than producers. There is no denying, however, the critical position they occupy nor the consequences their decisions have for independent producers.

This chapter explores this critical relation through the eyes and experiences of the independents themselves. No doubt if approached through the eyes of some of the gatekeepers, a different interpretation would be offered. In a relationship informed by material and cultural interests, such disagreements are perhaps inevitable. What follows cannot simply be discounted as 'perceptions' however, even if granted significance in their consequences (perceptions are 'real in their effects'). There is more insight on offer here than that. What is offered by the producers' accounts and experiences provides an insight into some of the structural, systematic and institutional forces at work which, condensed in the moment of commissioning, combine to delimit and shape the production of minority programmes in specifiable ways. These collective accounts and testimonies, by no means entirely critical or unappreciative of the sometimes constructive role performed by commissioners, point nonetheless to systematic biases in the commissioning process. The chapter first considers general observations on the commissioning relationship and process before listening, in turn, to producers' more detailed comments about dealing with the BBC, an ITV company and, finally, Channel Four.

Some of the institutional hurdles confronting any would-be programme maker seeking a commission for the first time are spelled out by a producer in the following way:

> When you are talking about film and video, the doors are really tight, whether you're black, white or whatever. It's a very capital intensive field. The doors are very tight. The nature of the way the commissioning happens in the TV industry: they don't have the capacity to see everybody. They tend to go with the people that they know and people that they know can deliver the products. At the end of the day they are on a commercial footing so they have to think about those things. So I think there are some mitigating factors. But having said that, it comes all too easy to do nothing at all, which is what happens a lot of the time. So, it's partly to do with perception. It's also to do with the way the whole system is set up. The mechanisms by which you can begin to try and unlock the doors are skills that have to be learnt.

There's all this language that has to be learnt to begin to talk with the Arts Council and to talk to people like the BFI (British Film Institute). You have to learn a certain language to do that. Some of the organisations like the BBC or the BFI, it's like you have to understand how their system works and you have to sus out what kinds of things to say. You know it's their buttons that you have to push and they're not really that interested in what you've got to say or your films. We were discussing this the other day, about how slot driven TV is these days. It's becoming so slot driven these days: you've a great film but no one's going to make it unless it fits in with their slots. They're just not going to make it. (Producer)

Entry into the world of commissions evidently is not a straightforward matter. It's highly competitive, commercially informed (if not driven), and it involves established networks. It also requires the acquisition of a new language, the language of television deals based upon a knowledge of how television commissioning works and the sorts of things the commissioning institution is interested in, particularly in relation to pre-determined schedule slots. As the producer says, these are considerable skills - skills that the experienced practitioner may more readily be able to deploy than the inexperienced newcomer. It is not simply a matter of experience alone however. Considerations of company scale or size come into play, as can established networks informed by tried and trusted professional relationships.

The present context of independent production has been shaped by the development of Channel Four as a programme 'publisher' in the early 1980s; by the subsequent growth of the independent sector, stimulated by broadcasting deregulation, and especially the 1990 Broadcasting Act and its stipulation on all major terrestrial broadcasters, including the BBC, to commission at least 25 percent of their original productions from independents; and, finally, by new technological developments in systems of television delivery, cable and satellite TV. Encouraged by economic rewards and new creative possibilities, numerous former in-house producers set up their own independent production companies in this period. What they retained were professional and personal contacts with the major television institutions. Small wonder, perhaps, that so-called 'sweetheart deals' between these former in-house producers and in-house commissioners should characterise the field of programme commissioning. As one producer explains:

> What happens, you get these BBC producers right. All of a sudden it's like independents get commissions, so they quickly drop the BBC and become an independent company and, all of a sudden, they get commissions. So that's the way it's worked. Even with Channel Four, a lot of people criticise Channel Four for using a lot of independents who were ex-TV producers and who had big production companies that had the ability. And the smaller independent production companies didn't get a look in. ...You have a whole load of built-in disadvantages against what you might describe as the 'true independents'. (Producer) (1)

It is commonly known for example that the first ever Commissioning Editor for Multicultural Programmes at Channel Four commissioned London Weekend Television (LWT), not independents, to produce two new flagship programmes, 'Black on Black' and 'Eastern Eye', in the early 1980s. Both Farruhk Dhondy, later in the same commissioning role, and Narendhra Morar, until recently head of the BBC's Multicultural Programmes Department, have also argued publicly 'that they are under no obligation to provide production work for black-owned companies, and that they have no responsibility to develop a black independent sector' (Salem, 1995, p. 71). All the producers interviewed were critical of the system of commissioning and its apparent privileging of major independents, some speaking at length about the prevalence of 'sweetheart deals':

And maybe there's an expectation that you don't go to certain commissioners because you know what they're looking for already. They've decided who they will take from. (Producer)

The more and more you see, the more experience that I have, I'm tempted to feel cynical about a lot of these things. I've seen the way their deals operate. Seeing the ways the power structure operates, the more incredulous you feel. 'We're commissioning more independents and I can't understand how you haven't managed to get in there!' It's quite easy really: because it's locked up between four or five major production companies! And if you do get information, it's an outside chance. Because the chances are, people in those four big independent companies probably worked with the commissioning editors for ten years, worked on different productions, worked at the BBC together et cetera, et cetera. I would add this as well. The first time that we got any joy at Channel Four was when we used this same strategy. We thought, right! We went out and found ourselves a producer who we knew was on the inside. Got him to be interested in the project that we were making and that, funnily enough, opened doors for us. ... You have to have talent for them to want to deal with you. But the point is this. There is actually a hell of a lot of people out there with talent: white, black, yellow, brown or whatever, a lot of people out there with talent who don't get the opportunity to pitch their ideas. (Producer)

This producer is apparently under no doubt that, in order to secure commissions under unfair competition, you must develop and use influential contacts, a practice that has apparently, in this instance, borne fruit. Of course, he may have been mistaken; he may have won his commission on competitive merit alone. But that is part of the problem in an industry in which 'sweetheart deals' and networking are apparently common practice and in which commissioning, by its very nature, takes place behind closed doors. It is difficult, if not impossible, to ascertain what really goes on. All too easily such a system can lead not only to cynicism, but also to suggestions of racism, though this charge was in fact made relatively rarely by the independents interviewed:

> Sometimes I wonder if they are being racist because there are all these minority groups entering the business. ... If they are not being racist they would help us in producing these things. (Producer)

More unanimously, the producers interviewed are under no illusion that major established independents maintain their position through unfair advantage. They also voiced suspicions that, on occasion, many commissioners were working to a relatively homogeneous view of the black audience and its programme needs.

> Let me talk not only as a programme maker but as a viewer. I wonder sometimes whether the people who are commissioning, maybe not just for ethnic or black programming, whether they really have a map or a real picture of the make-up of a black audience. There is still this feeling of, if you have one black programme, if you have one black series, you could address us all. It is patently nonsense. We are as complex as any society; there are young people, older people and so forth. ...They need to look again at the understanding, or a new map, or a new picture, of what the black audience is all about. (Producer)

Some producers also voiced strong suspicions that commissioners patronised both black producers and black audiences through occasional token programmes:

There's the complete (reaction) like, 'we haven't
been nice to that lot in St Paul's, let's tick them off
the list'. I wasn't born here, but I'm black so I'll do.
And to some extent you just think, 'Well if they want
to play that game I'll play too'. That's one way to get
money, but it's not a good way to get money. I get
fucking mad about it but that's the way it is at the
moment. (Artistic Director)

The same producer also drew attention to perceived sexism in her
experiences of the commissioning process, as well as a 'shopping
list' approach to identity politics and programme commissions:

We're three black women so that gets us an interview; it gets us through the door and it also gets us
quite a lot of tokenism. But it doesn't always give us
the money and it doesn't give us particularly big
money. I think you just get very cynical about it after
a while. I think there is a lot of big money around.
But the trouble with identity politics is, I think the
way the big organisations look on it is, 'Oh we've
done some black women last year, so we can't do you
this year'. Or, 'Well, you know, we've done that one',
and I find that really depressing. (Artistic Director)

While the general comments on the experience of dealing with
commissioners have tended to be negative, some producers have
also recognised certain benefits from the expansion of the independent sector. One producer also pointed to the potential role that
commissioners could play in convening a more general and open
forum in which the shifting sands of cultural change could be
discussed, and producers and commissioners alike could redefine
their priorities and interests:

...it's a good thing, because even if they are going to
ex-BBC producers, at least they are technically

functioning as independents and that means there is hopefully more space for camera people, runners, people who want to eventually be writers and directors and get work on high calibre projects. (Producer)

I'm not saying it's an easy life being a commissioner - I am happy to have a dialogue with a commissioner, even a general dialogue, and I think maybe we are still looking for forums as programme makers. ... We have very few forums to discuss our work. There needs to be an on-going dialogue with the commissioners because they can't know everything. ... You need a hundred eyes, people saying maybe the landscape has changed out there, and having an opportunity to say to the commissioner: 'Look I would suggest it's shifted'. ..... It's talking it through. ... That forum doesn't exist. I know that people have tried, but I am not sure we have succeeded in creating that breathing, living forum. (Producer)

Experience of dealing directly with the BBC was confined to the established, formerly in-house, independents interviewed. These have already commented above on the general problems of 'sweetheart deals' and so on which apply equally to the BBC and the ITV sector, a theme also pursued in Chapter Five in its discussion of the internal process of 'commissioning' in-house and independent programme productions for the Multicultural Programmes Department. As one producer reminded us:

Working as an independent it is hard to get money, but working inside the BBC you are working full time and this has its own constraints, and also not everything that you develop inside the BBC gets made either. (Independent and former BBC Producer)

Following upon the recent enforced expansion of independent productions for the BBC, an experienced producer observed how the BBC may in fact not be entirely 'geared up' for independent commissioning:

> My most recent experience has been with the BBC and my perception is that there is a split between the people who commission and the people who give money. The system is still trying to accommodate the fact that it is becoming more of a publishing house rather than a programme making institution. I think there is still some resistance to independents and there may be some feeling of 'We don't know how these people work', especially when dealing with black programme makers. (Producer)

Producers have already commented upon the deficiencies of regionally based ITV companies and their programming for minority ethnic communities, a finding previously examined in the author's study of Central Television PLC production based in Birmingham and its regional news and regional programme representation of ethnic minorities (Cottle, 1993a, 1993b). An illustration of the kinds of contact made with a regional independent television company is provided below. Based in Bristol, two producers repeatedly sought to gain commissions from Harlech Television (HTV), the major ITV regional broadcaster also based in the city. They recounted their stories at length:

> We've approached HTV on a number of occasions and HTV have been quite problematic for us because that understanding that I'm talking about with Channel Four, they don't have it at HTV. When you talk about black programmes to HTV, they just don't understand. I remember one very notable meeting that we had at HTV, where we were talking about making a documentary. It was basically about the roots of the

Rastafarian tradition in African rituals. It was a piece we wrote for something else and we put it to HTV. Anyway, they were considering actually funding it, but over conversation with one of the producers, it became really clear to us that they saw what we were doing as very much experimental for them. Not in terms of content, but just in terms of the fact that we were black film makers. Now that's really hard to deal with because they see what you are doing as necessarily 'other' just from the fact that you are black. (Producer)

We've dealt with HTV on several levels. HTV - it's difficult slagging people off, because at the end of the day we're going back to them. There's a quote in my diary which says, 'It's difficult to know which bridge to cross and which to burn'. ... It's difficult for us to break into the structure of HTV because they have no remit for the black community at all. I don't think they have any plans to bring in the black community in terms of their programming. I mean, you sit down and watch a whole heap of HTV and you don't see anything that's representing the black community unless they go down to St. Pauls and do a drugs bust or there's been a mugging. That's the only time they ever come down here. They don't really want to come down and find out what's really happening. They send us little bits and pieces saying, 'We really want to do this, yeah we really want to do that', but they don't ever come down with any sure plans which say, 'Right, you're a black organisation, let's develop some projects together. Let's get this thing going'. They don't really want to know. ... Coming from Birmingham, I think they had a bit more sensibility of the black community there because there's a major black community in the Midlands. It just makes me feel frustrated. If this is your local TV station, then, are they taking you seriously or are they still looking at you as experimental? What's the way forward for black film makers, black programming in this region? (Co-ordinator)

If unproductive dealings with certain ITV companies, such as those described above, confirm the producer's view of the necessity to break into regional broadcasting and make improved programmes for regionally-based minority ethnic communities, not all contacts with television institutions have proved to be so negative. Channel Four was often singled out for considered praise:

We do submit for those opportunities and, as yet, we haven't had any luck, but we do get feedback, particularly from the ideas that we submit to Channel Four. They do respond and hopefully in the near future we will make a breakthrough. (Training Co-ordinator)

I have to say Channel Four, they've been really good actually in all my dealings with them so far. (Producer)

Complaints of a perhaps unavoidable nature (though disproportionately coming from small independent companies) have been voiced, as in the following:

What I really resent is that you have to fill in so many bloody funding forms and they are so time-consuming, and you think, 'Am I doing film, or am I doing bureaucracy?' (Artistic Director)

Even when programme proposals have been turned down, it is apparent that Channel Four has put prior effort into information dissemination, followed up by lengthy discussion and feedback with applicants - even if, as far as some disappointed producers are concerned, the feedback rings hollow:

> In the past Channel Four has put out a lot of information and material to independents like myself telling us how independents like New Image can apply for them to commission a programme, and if you read their material they tell us that they aim to commission a lot of minority productions. But in fact when I have contacted Channel Four and tried to get some money out of them to do it, they have spent a long time reading our ideas and telling us that our ideas are good, but they don't deliver the money. They don't deliver the money. They talk one thing, but they don't deliver when it comes to putting the money on the table. And I've been frustrated, because they make the right noises. They make the right noises and tell us how wonderful we are and how important we are to the broadcasting picture. But they don't deliver the goods with the money. So a few times we have been frustrated with Channel Four. And we have found that, when they want to deliver something, it's for a project which they want us to make which we're not really interested in. We're not really interested in the emphasis that they have. (Producer)

> We've got Channel Four contacts and they're always saying how much they love our work and they'd like to see it on, but you know, it's like 'Well, come up with the goods, girls'. We have had research money. We did get some research money, but in the end they didn't take it on because they said they'd completely redesigned their programming and they were terribly sorry, but they didn't think our programme for young black women exactly fitted, and they also said it was a bit too black. So I got really fed up with them. But

you have to play the game. (Artistic Director)

The original remit of Channel Four was widely interpreted as a mandate to encourage the production of programmes for minorities. However, as senior editors have pointed out, the 1980 Broadcasting Act, setting out the remit of Channel Four, did not mention the word 'minority' but rather 'tastes and interests not otherwise catered for'. In other words, the interpretation is less specific in that 'minority' is inflated to encompass 'anyone who, at the time you transmit a programme, does not belong to the biggest group in the audience' (Docherty, Morrison and Tracey, 1988, p. 56). Nonetheless part of the original animating spirit of Channel Four, as well as its public perception, was for it to encourage and pursue programming for ethnic minorities, an expectation all the more likely to be disappointed when programme ideas are rejected:

> I applied to Channel Four and I was turned down. I was so disappointed knowing that Channel Four is a station for minority groups and, being a minority producer, I applied to them and I was very disappointed. (Producer)

While Channel Four is not exempt from producer criticisms, it is clear that it has managed to impress many with its degree of understanding and evident response to black independent producers. Of course, the fundamental nature of the commissioning process here, as elsewhere, is characterised by the commissioners' interests and general views and expectations of minority ethnic programming:

> The danger, especially with Channel Four, is that you are still worrying about whether you are targeting specific commissioners, and what those commissioners are looking for and their perception of what black broadcasting is about. (Producer)

Published views from Channel Four's commissioning editors have revealed how their expectations of black programming are indeed informed by particular judgements and an estimation of what television is capable of. Farrukh Dhondy, Commissioning Editor for Multicultural Programmes, has gone on record, for example, as saying, 'As a commissioning editor you have to ask: is this interesting, or is it simply somebody trying to get something off their chest - which I don't want'. Furthermore, as a self-proclaimed realist, he maintains that 'television is an industry not wish fulfillment', arguing, 'By and large what television should do - and that is why you require an editorial mind to do it - is to make a very humble judgement of what the country needs and do that' (cited in Docherty, Morrison and Tracey, 1988, pp. 58-9). Of course, though the judgement may be said to be 'humble', it is no less consequential for would-be producers seeking programme commissions, and for audiences. The ebb and flow of the cultural politics of 'race' and ethnicity and, importantly, the stance taken to this by programme commissioners, can prove decisive in commissioners' relationships with producers. This is not the place to pursue further the changing commissioning editors' views at Channel Four, and elsewhere, on the aims and forms of minority ethnic programmes; there is no doubting, however, the critical dependency of producers upon commissioners in this respect.

Even in the relative and imperfect terms of British broadcasting, it remains the case that most of the independents interviewed acknowledge, and occasionally praise, the distinctive efforts of Channel Four in its dealings with them. A final account of one producer's dealings with Channel Four gives a sense of the supportive culture provided and what this has meant to a newly formed, emergent production company. Interestingly, he also raises the possibility of a change in editorial regime as possibly working in his favour, but nonetheless remains appreciative of Channel Four's evident understanding of, and commitment to, the production of minority ethnic programming:

> I've dealt with Channel Four both in terms of exhibi-
> tion work and in terms of production work, and they

became one of the funders of the film festival that we ran. And that was incredibly easy to sort out. They were just in to it and they understood why we were doing it and they said: 'Yes, fine. Here is some money towards it'. And I promise you that was really astonishing at the time because we'd had so much trouble with so many organisations and some of the other people that you would expect would perhaps be a little more into the kind of work that we were doing around representation, around projecting positive images of black people et cetera. In terms of production, again they were really on the ball. We went to them with a proposal. You know, they have tried to assist us at every stage. We were in production at the time that we went to them. We created a proposal around the idea that we had. And they were very positive. Lots of advice, lots of contact, very accessible. Umm, I don't know, I mean I could be slightly cynical about this, because at the time when we wrote to Channel Four, there was a change of regime at the time. So I guess they were looking for their clients. It was a new regime and they wanted to create their own thing. They were very interested in attracting a number of new film makers to the independent film and video department, because many people perceived there had been certain log jams with the same kinds of film makers getting the same kinds of work off that department and not a lot of new blood coming in. So I think the time was right if you like. But they were very accessible to us. As a film maker, talking about a project, I think from the time I started in film I've gradually learned the language of talking less and less about the film and more and more about the kinds of things they want to hear. Whereas in Channel Four I could talk about the film and they understood what I meant. They understood the difficulties. They understood the problems and they were all kind of relaxed about it. It was kind of 'Yes, okay. Go away, have some development money, sort it out'. So far it hasn't seemed like a delaying tactic - they've been very, very helpful. (Producer)

Summary

This chapter has examined, from the producers' perspectives, the critical relation of dependency on programme commissioners and the numerous difficulties encountered when seeking to prise open the doors to programme commissions. These include the highly competitive environment of independent producers and the perceived weighting of the system towards those larger, more experienced and formerly in-house producers who now dominate the marketplace of independent programme production. Other factors identified include the necessity of learning the 'language' of programme deals and becoming attuned to the sometimes subtle, sometimes evident, nature of the programmes sought by commissioners - requirements that have changed through time. Also, how to address schedule 'needs' and reflect the commissioner's particular stance in relation to the shifting sands of minority ethnic *and* majority ethnic cultural politics.

If the acquisition of a professionalised television language draws attention to a form of 'cultural capital', differentially distributed across experienced and inexperienced producers, so the complexities and contending positions on the cultural politics of representation and its surrounding cultural political field also point to the exchange value of a more ethnically attuned 'cultural capital'. Producers have drawn attention to the need to monitor and pitch their programme bids in terms consonant with the particular commissioner's latest thinking on the needs of schedule slots and the wider play of cultural politics. Sometimes producers have found the informing agenda of concerns to be narrow, superficial and patronising, both to themselves and their audiences. On the other hand, some acknowledge-

ment of the institutional dilemmas and difficulties confronting commissioners has also been made, as have the occasional benefits of
working through ideas with them.

With specific reference to the BBC, producers have observed how
the enforced use of increased independents has still to be fully
integrated into the BBC's institutional mechanisms and ethos. The
regional companies of the ITV system were also discussed, with a
detailed account by a local independent of his contacts with HTV, a
major regional ITV company. Here the identified problem appeared
to be the distinct absence of minority ethnic 'cultural capital', or
understanding, on the part of HTV and its lack of commitment to the
minority ethnic audiences in its region and beyond.

With reference to Channel Four, the producers collectively recounted a more positive, though by no means entirely uncritical,
range of reflections and experiences. Channel Four's efforts in
distributing information about possible programme commissions
and details about the general commissioning process, as well as
follow-up support and guidance, were widely acknowledged. For
some, disappointment over Channel Four's rejections of their
proposals was felt particularly keenly, given the widespread expectations of the Channel and its commitment to minorities. Once again,
the inherent nature of commissioning, with its often opaque
programme expectations and schedule needs, confronts programme
makers as a constantly changing obstacle, limiting their own aspirations to professional and cultural independence. The continuing
importance of Channel Four in providing financial assistance and a
supportive culture was also illustrated in the appreciative tones of
one emergent producer. To what extent independent producers hope
Channel Four and other television institutions will provide them
with a programme making future is documented in the following
chapter.

Notes

1 The perception of this producer, and others interviewed, appears to contradict the available evidence about Channel Four and its commissioning of a large number of small independents and production companies, and therefore deserves comment.

Tables 10.1 and 10.2 below summarise Channel Four's use of independent companies, the numbers involved and the financial payments and numbers of programmes made.

Table 10.1
Programme payments and number of companies

Programme Payments	Number of Companies 1995	Number of Companies 1994
0 - £100,000	318	335
£100,001 - 250,000	94	100
£250,001 - £500,000	44	46
£500,001 - £1,000,000	30	28
Over £1,000,000	41	30
	527	539

Table 10.2
Number of programmes per company

Number of Programmes per Company	1995	1994
1	346	374
2 - 5	152	131
6 - 10	21	26
11 or more	8	8
	527	539

Note: The table above includes longrunning strands of programmes as one programme series. The *Brookside* series, of which three episodes are transmitted each week, is therefore shown in the table as one series. Source: Channel Four, 1996, *Report and Financial Statements 1995*, p.30.

The producer's perception and experience may not necessarily be mistaken however. Given that these commissioning features do not reveal the involvement of ethnic minority producers and production companies, nor the possible differences of average company financial commissions and numbers of programmes made by ethnic minority producers in comparison with others in the mainstream, it is possible that important differences may remain concealed in the tables above. The lack of effective monitoring by Channel Four makes systematic description and analysis impossible - a situation also criticised in relation to the BBC in Chapter Two.

11 Changing times

This last chapter of Part Two briefly considers the producers' views on the future of independent production. In so far as their views are informed by a practical understanding of, and intimate acquaintance with, emergent trends and the latest developments in the broadcasting scene, they can be considered more than idle speculation or crystal ball-gazing. They may, in fact, prove to be more or less prophetic. Together they identify worrying developments relating to wider changes in the structures of broadcasting and how these look set to impact upon the possibilities of increased and/or enhanced minority ethnic programmes. They also, perhaps more optimistically and speculatively, draw attention to the uncertainties and possibilities that globalization and the new communication technologies promise for minority ethnic audiences configured across the globe.

When asked what they consider to be some of the most important issues confronting producers of minority ethnic programmes both now and in the immediate future, they were quick to contextualise their views in relation to the wider changes affecting broadcasting:

> The whole future of broadcasting is up for grabs. It's about survival - and I don't know what's going to

happen. I'm sure that there will be a generation that will be successful in a while, but I'm on the cutting edge of something and I'm not sure that I'm going to survive. Why? Because it's very hard at the moment. There's going to be a generation of black people in this country, as there is in the States, who come through - if you look at television in the States now - it totally transforms black people everywhere in all kinds of positions - that hasn't happened in England at all. Whether it's going to happen in my generation, I don't know. I think it will happen maybe in a while, but you look at what the BBC is producing now, that's what they are going to be producing for the next five years. Black people do not feature in it. Black programming, black voices - forget it. (Producer/Director)

This former BBC producer, and now relatively successful independent, provides a fairly gloomy analysis of things to come. Notwithstanding her considerable track record of major commissions with the BBC, she feels poised on the edge of change and apparently fears her production company may not survive. Her view of the BBC and its current diet of black programmes, the diet for the foreseeable future, speaks for itself. In response to the same question, a slightly more wide ranging analysis is provided by the following producer:

I think that cannot be isolated from the general climate within the industry. Those pressures that particularly bear on producers from minority backgrounds are in a sense subsidiary issues because the main issues remain the same. That as television has been deregulated and continues to be deregulated, I think the issues of audiences and audience ratings have become very important. Therefore, there is all this push towards the common denominator and that

155

obviously does affect quality. But I really think the issue of 'quality' is no longer an issue really, given the development of new production technology; it's no longer about the quality of picture. I think it is about the quality of the programme offered. It is about the cultural and artistic content of the programmes offered. And my feeling is that it equally affects black producers.

Some element of public broadcasting I think has to be maintained. I think the BBC is very crucial in this. Channel Four's charter I think again is very important in this. The move towards wider audience appeal shouldn't really do away with some of the important aspects of public broadcasting that have continued to bring us an element of minority programmes and opportunities for black producers, black journalists, black presenters et cetera. I think that's an important issue. The BBC charter, Channel Four's charter, is equally important here. Because within that general social responsibility for publicly-spirited broadcasting also exists the notion for satisfying minority audience tastes and bringing diverse voices and diverse cultural programming from different sections of the community. So I think the threat is there; the threat would increase with the development of new distribution media. The call for deregulation of the BBC would increase. It is important to hold onto that aspect of what we have in terms of public broadcasting, both within public debate and in campaigning situations. (Training Co-ordinator)

Clearly this producer is in no doubt about the impact of the changing regulatory and commercial environment upon programme production in general, and minority ethnic programmes in particular. The fate of both are intimately related to the increasingly competitive pursuit of audience maximisation, a commercial imperative that threatens to undermine programme quality and established public service obligations and responsibilities. The BBC and Channel Four, though both under threat, are thought to have a crucial responsibility in holding the line and safeguarding at least some of the space, some of the representational opportunities, for minority producers and minority communities. This producer elaborates further on the consequences of these changes upon those spaces of representation, approached as programme forms, as follows:

> The second issue, which is a kind of flipside of that, is that de-regulation and the rush for wider audience share tend to bring with them a particular style of programme making which is the infusion of programming of whatever type, whether it's news, current affairs or drama, with elements of sensationalism, with elements of voyeurism. ... It also means that the kind of programming that is gaining a stronger foothold is of the usual type, the popular cheap game shows and chat shows and so on. I think these formats are not necessarily by themselves sensational; they are not by themselves necessarily anti-intellectual. But I think the challenge really is to try and look at these formats and try and infuse them with serious cultural content. And that as a whole is not just a struggle for black film makers but is a struggle for film makers and programme makers of any kind. (Training Co-ordinator)

The changing use of programme forms is here said to be directly related to the changing broadcasting environment. In the comments heard so far, especially those relating to the cultural politics of representation, with one or two exceptions surprisingly little was heard about the various representational possibilities of different programme forms. Commentary, in other words, has tended to focus upon the politics of subject matter or programme content. And yet, much of the excitement surrounding black independent film in the

157

recent past, at least within the academy and its close environs, has tended to be concerned with questions of experimentation and innovation at the level of form. Representational forms can, of course, also be approached as inherently political concerns in so far as established conventions of, say, dramatic narrative and documentary realism become subverted or reconfigured in ways thought appropriate to the film maker's subject (Mercer, 1988). The contemporary broadcasting conjuncture, however, is thought to allow little room for creative experimentation and innovation at this level. In fact, things are moving in the opposite direction.

The range of established and conventionalised television forms is under increasing pressure, with popular and populist programming threatening to further marginalise or transform serious formats. To what extent these formats are capable of being infused with more 'serious cultural content' is perhaps the ultimate challenge for any producer constrained to work in an increasingly commercialised, ratings-driven marketplace. This challenge, then, constitutes perhaps a second front in the engagement with considerations of form. If the first front, lined up against the aesthetic principles of 'documentary realism' and sought to 'reflexively demonstrate that the film, as much as its subject matter, is a product of complex cultural construction' (Mercer 1988: 11), so the second front may now be forced to engage, from the inside as it were, popular formats on the terrain of popular television culture. Some of the most recent developments in black programming suggest that producers have already taken up positions within the terrain of populist formats - not that this necessarily meets with approval from other independents:

> 'Zoo TV' - that's the buzz word these days we all want to talk about. Which is why things like 'Bad Ass TV' were made. Zoo TV is our kind of market/ theatre. And this is what people are beginning to talk about, in the same way they used to get hot about experimental work. ... Output has gone from being that very avant-garde, innovative, challenging work; it's just gone down the tubes into this kind of

commercial, tokenistic blending between the experimental and the commercial. Only as experimental as
is it is commercially viable, which by definition
doesn't really make a lot of sense. I'm not so bad in
that I've not been around as long as some of those
people have, and there are a lot of people in innovative TV who really have got nothing good to say
about Channel Four. (Producer)

Channel Four is an obvious point of reference and concern in this
regard, given its remit to innovate in form as well as content. Recent
changes in its funding arrangements and discerned commercialism
are not thought to bode well for the future however:

You do begin to worry if their vision of the plurality
of voices is now to be able to make commercial, not
very well thought out, sexually titillating programmes. It's not crap, because it's fun; it's like
'Eurotrash'; it's like fun but it's nothing. It's really
not going anywhere. Channel Four is going through a
bit of an identity crisis at the moment. ... I don't know
what will happen and I don't know where the spaces
will go, but I am worried. I don't think the spaces are
as open as they were in the 1980s. Films, programmes, they have to pay their way. Funnily
enough, I think the BBC might just emerge to be a
better home for black film than Channel Four,
because they have got this security and they can sit
back and say, 'Well, actually, we have got the money
to make these programmes, and we have got the
money to make programmes that are not necessarily
going to sell in this way. We can take those kinds of
risks.' I know that the BBC is producing several
drama pieces, black drama pieces under the Black
Screen initiative, which they are doing currently at
the moment and will continue to do so for some time.

I just think, the more commercial it gets, the harder it's going to be to unlock those funds. The kind of arguments black film makers were using around representation, around equal opportunities, I don't think anyone wants to hear them any more. (Producer)

If the future with regard to the major terrestrial television companies, including Channel Four, is generally thought likely to be increasingly restricted for minority programme makers and their output, at least some optimism is found on the global horizon. As one producer explains:

I think the new programme ideas, new ways of bringing forward stories, is a key issue and in this era of de-regulation I'm sure black programme makers are as equipped as anybody to enter the arena and come up with the type of programming that really will constitute the broadcasting of the future in a very competitive environment, both in terms of media and in terms of the new distribution media. Because we are now talking about cable, satellite and maybe in the near future we will be talking about the Internet as well. Don't forget there are still hidden markets out there that I think cry out for black programming. Not necessarily minority programmes, because I think the internationalisation and the globalisation of the distribution network means that, really, programme makers anywhere will be talking about minority ethnic TV programmes. Not in the narrow sense that we define in terms of a kind of national broadcasting network, but perhaps as an international broadcasting network where black programming will gain relevance, not just in Europe but also in Africa, in the

Caribbean, Latin America and within those conti-
nents and countries from which the minorities came.
(Training Co-ordinator)

In more pragmatic terms, the global scene is also thought to promise
the possibility of funding which is increasingly hard to find in the
UK:

> We're very aware that we have to think globally;
> these days we're thinking globally. We're not even
> thinking nationally, we're thinking globally about it.
> We're thinking about whether we can unlock some
> money from Africa, Europe, from the States. We
> have to make that level of activity which is obviously
> the opposite ends of the scale, but that is the only way
> that we know that we can be able to patch money
> together, to be able to make the kinds of projects that
> we need to make. (Co-ordinator)

The recent and promised developments in television delivery
systems - cable, satellite and digital compression - may indeed
reconfigure the nature of television broadcasting *and* narrowcasting
as discussed further in Part Three. America has witnessed the
success of the US cable network, Black Entertainment Television;
Identity TV (IDTV) was launched in London in 1993 and marketed
as Britain's first black entertainment channel, while TV Asia, a
satellite channel has been operating in Britain for some time
(Ismond, 1994; ITC, 1994). Real changes, then, are underway,
changes which promise to provide a service to Britain's minority
ethnic populations. However, whether these changes can be fully
embraced as representing a radical departure from, and alternative
to, mainstream television provision is a moot point. As Patrick
Ismond's detailed case studies of cable TV indicate, niche marketed
television is no less subject to commercial and competitive
pressures; if anything, those pressures may be felt more acutely,
undermining the production of original material and increasing the

reliance upon cheap entertainment imports. At present there is a general paucity of research into this whole area of new technologies, minority producers and minority audience involvement.

If, according to the independent producer above, the buzz word in television at the moment is 'Zoo TV', one of the buzz words in social science parlance is 'globalization'. This is not the place to rehearse the growing cacophony of voices contesting the respective interpretations and merits of this concept. Suffice to say, whatever 'globalization' is, most would agree that it is by no means a uniform or necessarily homogenising process. Contradictory and countervailing transnational tendencies are involved across the so-called 'global-local nexus'; the globe continues to be scarred by deepening divisions of wealth, resources and inequalities of geo-political power. In practice, 'global' rarely means world-wide, but rather specific international arrangements and interdependencies. The nation state is not yet dead. Moreover, assumptions about the development of a transnational black culture, perhaps premised upon the idea of shared diaspora histories or commonalities of experience and outlook, and sustained by new communication technologies, may turn out to be flawed. As recent critics of the cultural imperialism thesis have pointed out, beneath the surface of seemingly shared cultural commodities lies a busy subterranean world of cultural appropriation and sense-making, a world still in many ways fragmented and geographically and culturally compartmentalised. If the idea of a homogeneous black British culture has proved to be increasingly problematic, so the aspiration to a form of international or even global black culture and identity sounds increasingly improbable. This is not to say that visions of the future are wrong in identifying both the new communication technologies and processes of globalization as profoundly important developments, with direct bearing upon minority ethnic producers. They clearly are. Simply that their possibilities have yet to be fully understood, as have their contradictory tendencies.

Summary

This last discussion has identified a number of independent producers' recurring themes and concerns with regard to the future of minority ethnic programming and production. The changing nature of public service broadcasting in Britain has been identified by both established and emergent independents as holding little promise for improved minority production opportunities in the future. If anything, the independents claim to have witnessed the steady erosion of some of the gains won across the 1980s. Most worrying, perhaps, as institutions both Channel Four and the BBC are thought to have moved towards an increasingly commercial, competitive and populist approach to programming, tendencies that are thought to restrict and limit the opportunities for minority ethnic programme production. Confronted with this seemingly inexorable tide of change, some producers have been prompted to revisit considerations of programme form and formats. The inherently political nature of these, in terms of their representational possibilities, has been raised in the past by black film-makers. The challenge now confronting at least some black programme makers is how to 'go with the flow' and work within increasingly entertainment-driven formats and strive to shape them from the inside, introducing new content and tailoring them to minority interests, needs and viewpoints.

Finally, the possibilities heralded by new communication technologies and globalization were briefly alluded to and considered. In contrast to the BBC producers discussed earlier, it is interesting to observe how the community-based independents have generally tended to formulate a more panoramic future-oriented outlook, seeking out the possibilities of new media technologies operating within an increasingly deregulated and 'globalised' marketplace. The established independents already producing major commissions for the BBC and other broadcasting institutions were a little more pessimistic and cautious in this regard. Informed by the changing, and for them increasingly competitive and precarious, position of their production companies, they tended to see only tough times ahead. This position contrasts, in turn, with that of the BBC producers considered in Part One who, from their own institutional vantage point, offer perhaps the most pessimistic and inward looking view of the future. Here the institution of the BBC was felt to hold little future promise as far as safeguarding and encouraging minority programme production was concerned.

Though absolutely right to consider the fast changing possibilities offered by both new technologies and increased 'global' relations, a cautionary note on the assumed radical or alternative possibilities thought to inhere in these developments has been raised. Part Three of this study now takes up some of these themes with its more detailed examination of cable TV. To what extent the new communication technology of cable TV heralds a promising future for minority ethnic narrowcasting and production is explored in Patrick Ismond's two case studies of AsiaVision/AsiaNet and Identity TV.

Part Three
Circling the Perimeter Fence:
Cable TV Producers

It's a question of perception by the audience. How do they understand us? Do they understand our high ideals, or do they view us as just being 'Sky Television with a black face'? And I think we've got quite a long way to go. (Managing Director, AsiaVision)

12   From AsiaVision to AsiaNet*

Patrick Ismond

The TV producers consulted so far work within the 'perimeter fence' of the 'old' media. They either work within, or aspire as independents to work for, terrestrial television - BBC1, BBC2, ITV regional companies, and Channel Four. But what about those working in the 'new' communication delivery technologies and systems including satellite and cable? This study, in keeping with Cottle's research, attends to the aims, experiences and perspectives of cable operators and their efforts to service the needs of minority ethnic audiences outside of the traditional broadcasting terrain. The study is based on interviews conducted with media personnel engaged in cable television services targeted at minority ethnic groups.(1) Unlike most of the interviewees above, my interviewees perhaps represent more senior decision-makers and practitioners within the cable TV sector. Given the small numbers of personnel in my chosen organisations and their overall involvement in, and knowledge of, the production and selection of minority ethnic programmes for their respective cable organisations, they provide a useful vantage point from which to view the scene of minority ethnic cable television. The study

* This study is dedicated to my mother, and to 'Skip'.

draws on interviews with the Managing Director of AsiaVision and his successor in the renamed AsiaNet cable channel directed at Asian audiences, as well as the Co-Managing Director of Identity TV, a cable channel directed principally at an African-Caribbean audience.

The research complements the focus on independent and mainstream television producers. The 'new media' (cable, satellite) have a growing place in the British electronic media landscape, and are central to a national policy aimed at fostering competition in programme supply, and increasing 'consumer choice' (see for example Neil, 1982; Negrine, 1990). Minority ethnic services are an increasing feature of cable TV schedules, which currently include around 30 different services (ITC, 1996). Four of these are available from terrestrial television, and the other services are selectively installed, depending on the demography of a particular region. Each organisation was selected to give an insight into the opportunities and constraints attendant on minority ethnic narrowcasting (see below). Identity TV was at the start of its franchise when I conducted my study, whilst AsiaVision had been established for well over a year. Each, then, represented different stages of development and experience of surviving in the commercial cable TV sector. The interviews for this study were facilitated by semi-structured questionnaires using open-ended questions.(2) Semi-structured questionnaires have the advantage of allowing the interviewer to change either the wording of the question or the sequence in which they are asked, whilst open question formats encourage interviewees to answer questions as they choose. A tape recorder was used and interviewee responses transcribed.

The new media are important to this study because they promise new possibilities and, in this context, claims have often been made concerning their potential for enhancing minority ethnic representation. Cable, with its multi-channel capacity and ability to tailor specific services to discrete regions and communities, has often been viewed optimistically as the means by which the media's democratic base can be broadened (see Neil, 1982; Hollins, 1984; Fuller, 1993). Its promotion has often stressed cable's role as a showcase for domestic, local minority media production, and as a forum for diverse cultural expression. Narrowcasting, typically the function of distributing a range of television channels or programmes designed to meet various minority needs rather than to offer mass appeal is, then, the 'stuff' of cable. In the US, the use of cable's free access channel has been described as a stage for active, community-wide participation, and as providing a radically new kind of television. It also has a rich and 'stubborn' history (see for example Church, 1987; O'Huie, 1987; Fuller, 1993).

This study broadly follows the structure of presentation of the preceding discussion and is organised into two chapters. Two case studies, AsiaNet and Identity TV, form the basis of the two-chapter discussions, with each prefaced by background information on the particular cable channel - number of operating systems, backing partners and numbers of subscribers. In each case this is then followed by a section examining their respective aims, access and informing cultural politics of representation, followed by a section examining various structural controls, constraints and limitations. The following chapter also provides a general conclusion to this part of the study: a conclusion in which major findings and critical observations on the future role of cable as a provider of enhanced minority ethnic representation are outlined.

The case studies of AsiaNet and Identity TV, read together, paint a picture of the *narrowcasting* television environment aiming for minority ethnic provision in the commercial sector, circling the 'perimeter fence' of terrestrial *broadcasting* mapped out by Cottle above. The studies of minority ethnic television professionals working in the emerging commercial cable television sector thus help provide a more complete testimony of the experiences and constraints confronted by practitioners now working in a fast-changing television industry.

From AsiaVision to AsiaNet

Background Information

The AsiaVision channel was set up in 1986 by the cable company *CableTel*, operating in South and West London. The Managing Director's comments indicated that the decision to install an Asian channel as part of the 'basic'(3) package of services on select operating systems was motivated by commercial logic, rather than concern for minority media representation. He claimed that:

> They [CableTel] had just started to cable parts of Southall, which are predominantly Asian households, and they were finding a considerable resistance to purchasing cable TV. And they realised that in order to break down that resistance they had to provide some programming specifically for the Asian audience. So the Chief Executive...went to Bombay and bought some films...and he put those films on a separate channel...and that, in turn, increased the number of Asians who were buying Cable TV. (Managing Director)

The 'success' of this strategy, measured in terms of an increased take-up of services, gives some indication of the need for a service of linguistic and cultural relevance for this minority ethnic group.

At the time of interview, the cable service had survived one change of name and a further change of licensee and proportion of programme source (see later). Initially its original name, *Indra Dnush* (meaning 'rainbow') was changed to *AsiaVision* for reasons of clarity: people were apparently becoming confused by the numerous spellings of the word *Dnush* and the term's vague connection with the channel's specific minority ethnic focus. The name was changed to AsiaVision because:

> ...we wanted the 'Asia' bit to be prominent in it, but

we wanted the word 'vision' to have two meanings:
one, the meaning of television in the sense of broadcasting; and the one in the more philosophical sense
of vision.

Because we wanted people to realise that we had a
vision of a service that could provide something to
the Asian community. So that's how the name came
about. (Managing Director)

AsiaVision quickly developed from a service specialising in
imported Asian films to one showing game shows, documentaries,
news and sports. In 1993, the channel was re-licensed. AsiaVision's
successor, Asia Net, is based in the US and operates across the
whole of North America as a news and entertainment network of
cable, broadcast and satellite services. Broadcast in Hindi, AsiaNet
is available as a premium (or pay) satellite channel (4) and is
oriented towards 'affluent South Asians', most of whom own their
own homes and have annual incomes in excess of US$ 39,000
(AsiaNet, 1993). Since taking over the license in the UK, AsiaNet
has increased the total number of systems the channel is operating
on by 7 to 30; its subscriber count from 80 to 100,000; and, where it
is a pay service, its subscriber count from 3,500 to 5,000.

Aims, access and the cultural politics of representation

i) AsiaVision

What are the programming aims and objectives of AsiaVision?
Interestingly, AsiaVision did not have these formalised in, for
instance, a policy document. However, the Managing Director
claimed that:

The channel isn't aimed solely at Asians...it's not
Asians talking to Asians, and non-Asians keep out.

171

> We would like it to be seen as...the voice of Asians in
> the UK, where sometimes they would want to speak
> more generally to others.

According to ITC figures for 1993, this 'voice' attracted some
80,000 (Asian and other) subscribers (ITC, 1993). The Managing
Director estimated that between 70 and 80 percent of these subscribers were of Asian origin, and that virtually all Asians with the
channel viewed it at some point in the week, for 2-3 hours continu-
ously.(5) Within the audience sector, which sub-groups, differentiated by age, sex, religion and class, was the station aiming to reach?

> Part of the audience who are most keen on it would
> be the older generation, traditionalists, and quite a lot
> of the programming is aimed at them; but there are
> 'strands' which are aimed at the youth and children's
> audience. (Managing Director)

The programming emphasis of the channel, which is largely own-
language material set in, and concerning, the Asian sub-continent,
raises issues concerning its relevance to young Asian people attempting to make sense of their lives in Britain (as discussed later).
Does operating in the commercial sector impact on the provision of
programming for other Asian audience sub-groups? The Managing
Director's response in this respect was illuminating:

> Like any commercial television network, the vast
> bulk of the programming is aimed at attracting the
> vast bulk of the audience. When it comes to profes-
> sionals, they have different requirements...like *The
> India Show*, like *Newsview*, like sports programmes,
> that appeal to the more well-off part of the audience.
> And there are some programmes like some of the
> serials, some of the soaps, some of the gameshows,
> that appeal more to the downmarket part of the
> audience...there's something for everyone...But in

172

terms of attracting an audience from the socio-economic ABC1s, there is less material of that kind in the schedule.

To a certain extent because it is more difficult to find, it's more expensive and, in providing that material, you are actually attracting a minority within your minority.

With a reliance on income through advertising and sponsorship, audiences need to be 'delivered' in sufficient size or 'quality'. From a purely commercial standpoint, then, it is surprising that audience sub-groups, such as the professional middle class, were seen as too much of a 'minority within [a] minority', to provide a sufficient volume of programming for. The fact that the programming was seen as too expensive and difficult to acquire further emphasises the limits of the market in the provision of 'niche market' programming. By preferring to cater to more broadly-differentiated audiences, the Managing Director's conception of the role and aim of narrowcast minority appears more in keeping with the broadcasting model of mainstream television. In practice, a typical programme schedule ran as follows:

11:30 - 14:30	A re-run of the previous night's prime-time viewing, primarily for those people working 'shifts';
14:30 - 17:30	An afternoon 'classic' movie, primarily for the 'housewife';
17:30 - 20:30	Early 'peak-time' programming for the whole family: mainly serials, soaps, game shows and documentaries;
20:30	two 'back-to-back', 'premier' feature films. Designed to attract the maximum audience and working on the principle that the Asian target audience is seen to 'peak' later than its more hetrogeneous ITV/BBC counterpart.

The Managing Director claimed that this model had distinctively different programmes at different times of the day. In keeping with demonstrable realities, it sought to respond to the fact that many

173

female members of the Asian household, particularly mothers, spend large parts of the day at home, having sent the children to school. Also, mothers were seen as less inclined to go out by themselves, partly because of language difficulties. Where the male members of the household were working, this was understood to include a significant amount of 'shift-work': for instance, in restaurants and factories, and driving taxi-cabs. It is significant that in Bradford, a city with a high concentration of Asian people, these social and work patterns still apply (see for example Parvin, 1989).

The station's programme model is seen to follow the *public service* tradition of educating, informing and entertaining the viewer. However, in view of the channel's commercial imperatives, these themes assume a different priority:

> ...it's entertaining, informing and educating in that order. There is some educational programming for children...but entertainment is the primary aim of the channel because it's selling advertising, and it's selling subscription. The thing people most want to buy is entertainment. Information comes second in terms of feature programmes, documentaries, magazines; and education comes third. So we have a slightly different bias towards these three things but we still abide by these three principles. (Managing Director)

Entertainment, then, was perceived as the preferred choice of the consumer. Ostensibly, this can be supported by the success of US pay cable, with its promotion of first-run feature films and sports, and the recent success of *BSkyB* in the UK along the same lines. However, it raises fears about, *inter alia*, the global spread of de-politicised cultural products (see for example Williams, 1994; Chan, 1994). In this vein, an examination of the station's programming content suggested that its 'political' dimensions (programming concerned with minority ethnic unemployment, the effects of 'racism', government policies regarding immigration, et cetera), were largely unarticulated on the schedule.

174

Sources of entertainment for the channel were varied, but invariably imported from the Asian sub-continent. Independent production companies or commercial television channels in India, Pakistan, Bangladesh and Sri Lanka provided the bulk of the programming. Little was obtained from these countries' state television counterparts, but even less (at most 15%) from 'assorted sources'. According to the Managing Director, these included:

> ...independent production companies in the UK. There are a few things we make ourselves. We've just covered the Asian film awards; we make a magazine programme once a month called *Newsview*; we've done some cricket coverage, we've done some sports coverage; we've done the odd interview programme. But those things are made when we feel there is a gap in the market that can't be satisfied with an import.

The grant-aided local film and video centres around the country provide a rich archival source of work from aspiring producers, many of whom work on shoe-string budgets. Their thematic concerns attest to the variety of identities structured along the axes of class, race, gender, sexuality, or a confluence of these (see for example Hussein, 1994). It was significant, then, that the Managing Director's comments implicitly indicate the *ad hoc* nature and low priority that the channel assigns to domestic independent production. This point was made clearer by the Managing Director in relation to the local or regional infrastructure that the channel could use, to subsidise and promote writers from local Asian communities. He stated that:

> It's too small to honour it with that kind of grand description. But, we do have a sort of network of people we know. We have a couple of freelance producers who do make things for us, and who do instigate...I think *instigate* rather than *commission*:

175

commission always implies the exchange of
money...and we really are too small and too young to
spend amounts of money on commissioning things.
We do sometimes instigate projects that we do for
ourselves...so...for example, we might incorporate
into our monthly magazine programme a book review or a review of a stage production or a film, or
something where we would get in touch with a
freelance writer or a freelance journalist and ask
them to do that and present it...We wouldn't necessarily commission full works. We wouldn't necessarily be commissioning a documentary or a drama at
this stage. (emphasis added)

Attempts to cultivate the grassroots involvement of local community groups, at all stages of media production, is very much part of
the cultural politics of representation. It asserts the need for a
plurality of interest group involvement in media processes, as the
best way to create a system where consumers recognise themselves
and their aspirations as being fairly represented. The exclusion of a
volume of independent productions on the channel was partly due to
financial constraints, although the Managing Director's comments
also arguably indicate an absence of will.

He also entertained a conception of the role of the media in the
lives of Asian people, a vision informing the cable station's aims (if
not the reality) of service provision. He explained at some length
that:

Whether you accept it or not, there is no doubt that
the influence of television...is very, very considerable
in the light of everybody in this country. Now, it isn't
necessarily a good influence; it can be a bad influence. For young people, and especially young people
of a certain impressionable age, television does present a role model. It presents a kind of fictitious
lifestyle that they're encouraged to aim for. If that

lifestyle, which is all fantasy anyway...is entirely white, then it reinforces the message that being white is number one, and not being white is number two. But it goes further than that, because if that fantasy world and if those images are not just white but are English, then it also reinforces the message that to be English is good, not to be English is bad; to speak English is good, not to speak English is bad. Language reinforces this perception of the white image of desirability, because it enforces it not just with skin colour, it enforces it not just with culture...but it reinforces it in terms of language. And within the Asian community, there is a sense that young people feel that it's 'not done' to speak Hindi or Gujerati or Urdu et cetera...Television has a very considerable influence...Where there are programmes that feature black people, that helps to redress the imbalance and create a feeling that it is okay to be black.

The Managing Director's comments thus reveal a conception of the channel as a service that attempts to redress a 'cultural imbalance', expressed in terms of a dearth of Asian images and culture on television. It is not surprising, then, that the need to explore the many identities contained *within* the 'Asian' classification, appears to be subsumed under a desire to use the channel to promote Asian images and cultures *per se*. As we shall hear, this view contrasts with that of Identity TV's, in emphasising the *quantity* rather than *quality* of media images as of prime concern.

ii) AsiaVision to AsiaNet

In 1994, 18 months later, a change of licensee was accompanied by a new Managing Director and channel name, from *AsiaVision* to *AsiaNet*. The overall aims of the channel were said to have changed also. AsiaNet's Managing Director stated that:

Last year the management...were very good but not
right for the Asian programmes. Hence we had a lot
of problems. A lot of stuff a lot of people did not
understand what was to be portrayed to the Asian
public. Hence we had our problems...[the Managing
Director/Programme Supplier for the *Indra Dnush*
channel] again had no idea of Asian, ethnic backgrounds - alright he was...an elderly chap, so it's not
even that he had picked up a lot of ethnic, and media
and ethnic background knowledges or experiences
from day-to-day life. He didn't do that. Hence it was
very difficult for him to decide what or when to buy
and what programmes to show. Take AsiaVision.
The same thing happened. We had [AsiaVision's
Managing Director] - very good chap, very educated
and clever - but he doesn't have the Asian idea...He
had no experience of working with Asians or ethnic
people, hence they also did not know what to do
about it. They used to show rubbish on television
and, when somebody used to complain, they didn't
know whether it is rubbish or it's good.

The new Managing Director's sketch is crude in places and, at first
sight, he could be accused of simply 'slagging off' his predecessors.
And yet, the testimony of AsiaNet's Managing Director does address an important issue in the debate concerning the cultural
politics of representation. The sub-text of his testimony appears to
endorse the view that minority ethnic control of media processes is
important to accurately cater to the tastes of these audiences. There
is a sense here that both the former Managing Directors simply
bought 'Asian' films to show their audience without considering its
diverse nature. A perceived cultural barrier between the (white and
English) former Managing Directors and their Asian audience was
thus seen to account both for complaints about the station's content
and the failure to acquire more subscribers during the life of the
franchise. Even so, AsiaNet's Managing Director chose not to

predicate changes to the schedule on the basis of audience research, but on his 'intuition' about their cultural needs. It is contestable what credence should be attached to 'intuition' in catering for audience needs, though the Managing Director had been a programme supplier to various Asian cable channels in the US and the UK over the last twenty-five years. He was content to marshall the statistical evidence cited above, detailing increased take-up of services and operating systems, to support his claims.

So how would AsiaNet cater to diversity within the Asian audience? In the Managing Director's view:

> It is very difficult for them [Asian elderly parents] to change their ways and means now to learn enough English, to go out and mix with the local population. It's not possible, so hence it is our duty as a cable media to bring to them at home what they would like to see, but we don't want to make them into stones, into cabbages. We want to show them the changes also...We will do it in such a way that, first, we get them hooked onto the TV, and then start showing them media things like AIDS, like local problems, like local things in different languages, which is available now...Our next object in Leicester is to have more Gujerati, in Bradford to have more Urdu...to have more Bengali in Southall, to have more Punjabi and Gujerati. For people out there in Bradford we'd show you more of back home in Pakistan. [But] of Pakistan to people in Southall then, with the friction going on, then they'd switch it off. I'm not doing them a service. I'm actually creating problems. This is exactly why AsiaNet is different to AsiaVision.

The Managing Director's response to addressing diversity within the Asian audience appears to be structured principally along lines of age, with the provision of an own-language, regionally based service to initially alert people's attention to important social issues. The Managing Director's statement also highlights the need to recognise political divisions existing within the Asian communities. In so doing, it rejects the idea of this 'community' as being unified and/or homogenous - an important position in the wider debate on cultural representation (see for example Bygrave, 1994).

The channel's focus on elderly migrants, with provision of Asian - language programming, begs an obvious question, asked also in relation to AsiaVision: how relevant is this focus to the lives of Asian people born and living in Britain with no experience of Asia? In promoting this programming, the Managing Director saw as paramount a cross-generational, pedagogic link. In his view:

> It's the youngsters who were born here who are now 25, 26 years old. They have totally left, they are totally unaware of anything of India other than they are Indians born at home [in England]. Yes, that becomes very important to us as the media to educate those boys and girls, those youngsters with thoughts from the grandparents and with the blessing of the parents that this is how it works, this is how it was, this is how it affects us: and that's exactly what we're showing.

In relation to the sources of programming for the new channel, the ratio of imported to domestic production, and the *character* of the latter, have changed. According to the Managing Director:

> Seventy percent of our programming is imported today. Thirty percent we aim and we have managed to get local programming: which could be to do with local tourism, could be to do with medical issues, could be to do with local MPs, immigration issues, which are starting now, dance beats, Asian music in this country. So that's thirty percent we're using locally. Seventy percent is originated from India,

from Pakistan, from Bangladesh, and we are trying to get more from Sri Lanka. Our sources are from the Asian sub-continent...We want to do a lot of local programmes; we want to sponsor local programmes...we want to do regional programmes. According to us, according to me with my experience, the regional programming exists in Leicester, in Bradford, in Southall and in Brighton...We have got a program down in Wolverhampton. A gentleman has left us these 14 tapes and we've bought them. So indirectly we have sort of sponsored it for him...He's picked up the local Asian people who can sing, poetry-type songs...but before that, he showed what Wolverhampton wants, what Wolverhampton needs, and it's good. So we are encouraging local people-writers, musicians.

This is an encouraging view about cable TV and the involvement of local people and producers. But is it entirely accurate? AsiaNet is under similar financial constraints to other commercial cable stations, as discussed below. It too hopes to maximise audiences to attract advertising and sponsorship, as well as to allay investment fears by showing commercially 'safe', popular programming. The promotion of domestic independent production, which also included the search for in-house production facilities, was therefore a surprising contrast to AsiaVision's utilisation of the channel, and can only be welcomed. In spite of economic constraints, the Managing Director's conception of the channel's role resonated more closely with cable's use by local 'communities of interest', as a political or social vehicle, that was a part of its initial promotion. AsiaVision's narrowcasting potential was seen as a definite 'selling point' over an organisation like *TV Asia* (the equivalent satellite channel), which is technologically unable to de-massify its audience on such a small scale. Narrowcasting is nonetheless compatible with the notion of pluralism in representation and access. Its ability to generate subscriber interest, and attendant sponsorship, is a comment on the viewing needs left uncatered-for by mainstream broadcasting. The increased financial risk associated with this conception was in part reduced because:

> ...we [AsiaNet] have injected a lot of money, and we have to inject a lot more, hence we are at this situation today where...we are spending more time and money in looking for new premises, which will be adequate for a studio for lighting...

Controls, constraints and limitations

i) AsiaVision

Major controls, constraints and limitations identified by the cable operators in the provision of minority ethnic programming are now addressed. Discrimination on the grounds of 'race' continues to blight the lives of Britain's minority ethnic groups (see for example Smith, 1977; Jenkins, 1986; Gordon, 1990). Although physical violence and verbal abuse are its most blatant manifestations, there are other, more insidious practices, which have equally significant consequences. AsiaVision's Managing Director highlighted the way that social organisation and structure contributed to the institutionalised racism of the media industry, thereby constituting an important constraint on black access and representation. AsiaVision's Managing Director was white and male, but claimed to have always been aware of the harmful effects of 'racial' and sexual marginalisation in the media industry. In his view, these effects are perpetuated because:

> First of all there is the natural - you might call it unnatural, but it is perceived as natural - inclination on the part of white, middle-class, Anglo-Saxon, wealthy, successful men to appoint clones of themselves in jobs underneath. And I don't just mean in terms of the colour of their skin; I mean gender

182

clones as well. There are very few women working in senior positions in television for exactly that reason, so it's very much a chauvinism, as much as being a race thing. Also however, there have been up to now some reluctance on the part of some middle managers in television to put black faces on the screen...and their justification for that is often: 'Well I'm not prejudiced myself, but a large number of our viewers are, and we don't want to upset them'. Thereby of course, creating a vicious circle...I was always aware of there being an absence of a mixture of races in [regulatory] organisations, and I still think frankly that it's absolutely scandalous that bodies like the Independent Television Commission are staffed by white, middle-class Englishmen.

It is possible to challenge the easy assumption that the Managing Director makes concerning the (problematic) existence of 'races' in his understanding of the perpetuation and effects of racism. In a context of limited media access, AsiaVision's Managing Director also asserted a need to consider the 'mindset' of the few black individuals working in these environments; and whether, in the process of securing a media career, they may have been 'co-opted and contained' by the dominant value system:

Very often, the most successful people in the media who are black are then perceived by their brethren as coconuts.(6) Trevor MacDonald [black newscaster on ITV] is a very good example. Many people see him as being a 'coconut': white man inside. So sometimes you can't win. But I think sometimes black people, in order to be successful in the media, adopt white attitudes, which is' I don't think, a good thing to do at all. I think it's a real sell-out...in terms of dress or hairstyle...or, in women's cases...it can be playing-down some characteristic they might otherwise play up, in hair, make-up, dress, whatever. But I think very often, the media itself creates an atmosphere where people do these things without their immediate line manager...imposing them at all.

The Managing Director's comments concerning constraints on black personnel working within the media industry raise a number of issues regarding identity and culture. The political consequences attendant on black media personnel have been of concern for some time. For instance, it has been suggested that journalists working in the 'minority broadcasting units' at the BBC and Channel Four have actively colluded in perpetuating standards of 'culturally irresponsible' journalism associated with the industry as a whole (see for example Alibhai-Brown, 1994). In addition, feminist writers in particular are increasingly questioning 'essentialist' definitions of blackness. Essentialism seeks to legitimate black identity only if it speaks of certain cultural experiences and is linked to specific modes of being. The 'legitimating experience' encompasses linguistic accent, style of dress, musical tastes and political philosophy. In the case of Trevor MacDonald, the 'white attitude' that the Managing Director and other critics are referring to is his 'Oxford English' accent. Hooks (1992), however, would question the term 'a white attitude'. She would ask what it is about being black that means that one has to be 'culturally straitjacketed', and why someone cannot be aware of their black identity as expressed through a range of cultural practices (see also Hall, 1992; Gilroy, 1993a, 1993b). The Managing Director's testimony, then, appears to endorse a limited sense of minority ethnic identity, and this (commerical considerations aside) is arguably reflected in the discouragement of programming for 'minorities within a minority'. It is important, therefore, to recognise a combination of structural and ideological/cultural forces at work which determine controls on, and differences in, the provision of minority ethnic programming.

A closer look at the relationship between programming and sources of revenue uncovers more 'structural' controls and constraints on practice. In this regard, the Managing Director's comments are worth quoting at length, as they illustrate the dynamics of this relationship clearly. He claimed that:

> We have two basic sources of income, subscription and advertising. The income from advertising is much lower than it is from subscription, but it is significant income none the less. The constraint is on the number of viewers. Because any commercial television channel which is constantly reaching 80,000 viewers has to be deemed to be remarkably small. And when you're that size, beggars can't be choosers when it comes to buying television programmes. I will give you a couple of examples of things where the lack of access to the sort of money that ITV might have, for example, is working against us. One case is a cookery programme we run which was very popular. We wanted to buy the second series, but we could only show it after they'd shown it. Now, if we'd had more financial muscle, we could have said: 'No, no, no, stuff and nonsense, we had the first series, we'll have the second series, and you can show it second.' But clearly, the kind of price a small television station like ours pays is a lot less than the BBC because we're paying proportionally for the number of viewers we've got. But it also means that you don't have the muscle when it comes to negotiating exclusivity or first-transmission or whatever. Equally, there was a cartoon series we would have loved to have bought that was made in America, and the producer said, 'Well, they had actually invested so much money in this programme' that they couldn't afford to sell it to us for the kind of money that we, and indeed others in our kind of field, pay. So I think the kinds of programmes that we're most constrained from putting on the channel that we probably, all things being equal, would like to, are

very recently-made programmes because quite often we're buying serials and game shows that are several years old. So we don't have the 1993 [interview year]...quiz show. And the other thing we're constrained on is current affairs, topical programmes of that nature...We can't really buy them in from India because we want something that's relevant, culturally relevant to the UK, and we have to make it, or commission it, and that's too expensive.

As noted earlier, commercial forces are moulding the content of the channel towards cheap, imported entertainment programming. Programmes which were seen as more expensive to produce and with no 'shelf-life' - principally, the *current affairs* and some *documentary* genres - were virtually absent from the channel's schedule. Perhaps the complexities of this relationship between programme access and cost, more than any other, illustrate the limitations of the market in the exchange of cultural goods. This relationship will undoubtedly determine the fortunes of the cable channel, a point not lost on the Managing Director. In his view:

It's a question of perception by the audience. How do they understand us? Do they understand our high ideals, or do they view us as just being 'Sky Television with a black face'? And I think we've got quite a long way to go.

Intense competition for *advertising revenue* has a related effect on programming, as less money from this source will result in less being invested. In view of the age of some of the channel's programme offerings, it is hard to imagine the more prestigious advertisers competing for airspace. Nonetheless, AsiaVision's Managing Director saw the station as vying with Asian newspapers, magazines and radio for advertising revenue. In the delivery of audiences to advertisers, and for reasons of access to a greater range of programmes, competition lies with satellite television's news services and movies.

Further, related constraints concerned public perceptions of 'quality' and 'value' in broadcasting. The high production and broadcast standards set by mainstream television were seen as expensive to reproduce, but the channel was nevertheless expected to do so, as confirmed by AsiaVision's Managing Director:

> ITV, Sky, MTV, CNN. Big companies, lots of money. Spend a lot of time, money and effort on making their channels expensive, glossy, attractive, desirable. Because of the small number of viewers we have, we've got far less money to spend on these things and we are often berated by the Asian community for 'looking cheap'; and we look cheap, because we are cheap in comparison, and that is a very difficult one. We try very, very hard to try and replicate the look of an expensive channel on a very low budget. But sometimes what happens is, with the best will in the world and the best ideals in the world, you offer a service and you say: 'This is for Asians, this is an Asian programme service, this is catering specifically for the Asian community in terms of scheduling, in terms of programming'. There are quite a lot of our customers who look at it and say: 'But it's not nearly as good as *Sky One*. Why not?' And that's because, in this country, people are still accustomed to TV being a utility like a tap that you turn on and there's always water there, and it's clean, and it's fresh. And first of all they're being asked to pay quite a high price. And again, there is a price differential here, that in those areas where we are a premium subscription channel...to get us it's [say for example] £22.00. Well, actually, it's £22.00 to get 15 or 16 channels including us. Often the perception is that they're paying £22.00 a month just for us, and that they're not getting value for money. It's very,

very difficult to struggle against that kind of overwhelming competition, where that [English] culture
is perceived as being superior in the way it is being
presented...But I have every confidence that, in ten
years time, we'll look every bit as good as anybody
else does.

The economics of production again begs the question about where
'alternative' agendas should be screened: within a more expansive,
encompassing mainstream TV service, or as part of an (invariably
under-resourced) 'minorities' sector?

ii) AsiaVision to AsiaNet

Examining the relationship between programming and sources of
finance may reveal the extent to which it can disrupt the channel's
preferred programme schedule. According to AsiaNet's Managing
Director, the channel was not heavily reliant on the revenue gained
from advertising, sponsorship and subscriptions. However, he
claimed that:

...most of our finance is from outside finance. But we
would like to get more money from advertising. We
would like to get more money from sponsors. Yes,
we would like to get more money from cable subscribers. That is a very slow and long process, so we
can't run the station thinking that. But because we
have more numbers [subscribers]...we are attracting
advertising revenue and sponsorship...We are looking for it, and that is our main target.

Obviously, the additional revenue would help to cushion the channel
against the vicissitudes, the peaks and troughs, of the commercial
marketplace. However, funding *per se* can bring its own limitations:

There is a problem...and I say it does happen. We at

programming want to show a certain [programme topic] and we don't find sponsors or advertisers to back us on that...It happens most of the time...We want to show programmes on off-beat subjects in India, i.e., poverty, i.e., also on the reality of Indian events, on uneducated people in the villages. We want to show stories and we want to show serials based on them. Why? We don't want to show them...to show the world how poor India is, but it's to show to the world what the world can do for India. Unless people know what's wrong or what's right there, they won't know how to correct it...I have got programmes that I would like to show. I would like private organisations to back it up, the Government of India should back it up. They don't, they don't, like I said. And I do buy most of my programmes from India television centre to do with Asia...but instead of giving it to me for free, they charge me for it, even documentaries. So there are a lot of problems. (Managing Director)

This testimony indicates that AsiaNet was constrained by the lack of political will to support imported, issue-based programming. This finding is significant because it further emphasises the commercial *pull* away from 'serious', controversial current affairs programming, towards the entertainment focus of AsiaVision. High ratings, then, impose their own form of censorship.

AsiaNet's lack of money to self-finance specific projects is exacerbated by competition from other minority ethnic media. In this regard, the Managing Director claimed that:

There are two or three other centres...TV Asia is one, Namaste [both Asian cable channels] is another, and the third is us...I'm not saying TV Asia is big, but TV Asia and AsiaNet are an equal level. Namaste is nothing to compare to the two of us, it is only about

eight hours on the weekends, so is only giving weekend service. But we are giving 18 hours service all
day and over seven days. Hence it's lots of programming, lots of mistakes and a bit of good programming in that. TV Asia is a fresh company, open only
one and a half years ago. It's transferring to satellite,
although the same film which we show through cable
to VHS tapes...they just show through satellite and,
believe me, their quality is much better than
ours...People ring us up and tell us: 'Why is your
quality not very clear?' I can prove to the people, I
can prove to anyone, that some films, the same
master [copy] has been to TV Asia and we have got
the same master now but, because of the way we
transmit, it's bad. Hence competition is there.

The same concern about technical quality led the Managing Director's predecessor at AsiaVision to proclaim that the channel 'looked
cheap by comparison' to the major companies. Competition for
viewers will have a direct effect on advertising revenue for the
channel as well. In this regard, AsiaNet's Managing Director regret-
ted that:

We take a backward stand, we are not forward compared to TV Asia. TV Asia has got bigger budgets,
remember. This company [AsiaNet] has changed
hands three times, twice in the last three years. Hence
it makes a difference. So by the time we set up and
arrange everything again, the company gets sold out
and the new people come in and it makes a difference. TV Asia is a fresh company, it came up with
fresh policies, hence they are doing pretty well.

This statement seems to suggest that a level of company stability and
new ideas are required to survive in the volatile commercial sector.
This would presumably gain the confidence of advertisers, as well as

obviously enhance subscriber levels.

Finally, the Managing Director also drew attention to implications of regulatory control for the content of programming on the channel. In his view, the Independent Television Commission's (ITC) 'policing' role in relation to programme standards was not an area for concern. Sex was seen as traditionally 'indiscreet' in Asian broadcast, and violence was much less common than in Western (geography, not genre) productions. He claimed:

> AsiaNet...always shows programmes which will show the goodness and the good points of society...not entertaining people through violence...we want to educate people on cultural programmes and entertainment linked to that. We are happy that the ITC has imposed those restrictions.

This statement begs the question about the extent to which British Asian people, weaned on a Western diet of sex and violence in films, are likely to appreciate these offerings.

Summary

AsiaVision's programming schedule was heavily influenced by market forces. High costs were prohibitive to the acquisition of certain types of programming. 'Dated' entertainment was provided in the main for the largest audience sub-groups, whilst the smaller, less viable ones were less adequately catered for. The high cost and 'risk' associated with domestic production meant that the channel had no infrastructure to develop or commission unknown, local production talent, and so bypassed an important benefit of cable narrowcasting. By contrast, AsiaNet appeared to be investing in the facilities to produce programming in-house, as well as promoting locally-made programming for the channel. This focus appeared more viable for AsiaNet because of its greater finances. However, the interviews also made apparent the different conceptions that each

Managing Director had concerning the role of the channel in the lives of Britain's black population. Those too have also influenced the different uses that cable TV has been put to.

AsiaVision's Managing Director gave an even clearer indication of how, for minority ethnic audiences, a range of controls and constraints determine the reality of service provision in the commercial sector. In this vein, institutionalised racism in the media industry was seen to act as a constraint on minority ethnic access and practice. Funding was a sensitive issue for AsiaNet given that, in some cases, it was conditional on a move away from issue-based programming, and presumably towards the more entertainment focus of AsiaVision. The general scarcity of revenue for both channels was further highlighted by competition from other media outlets in an increasingly fragmented market. In this regard, it would appear that satellite television is winning an important war for viewers and advertising revenue, because of the superior quality of its transmission signal.

Notes

1 The interviews for this study were originally conducted for my recent (1994) PhD thesis, 'Ethnic Minority Media Production in Relation to British Media Policies', Bradford University. I would like to take this opportunity to thank my research supervisor, Professor Charles Husband, and my colleague at Bath College of Higher Education, Dr Simon Cottle. The latter's incisive and helpful criticisms of my drafts contributed in no small way to the final product that is these two chapters. I would also like to thank Jo Haynes for expertly and efficiently transcribing the AsiaNet interviews.

2 The original interview schedules were designed for the wider purposes of my PhD study and have not, therefore, been included in the appendix. The schedule used did invite responses, however, covering the broad areas of concern and interest addressed throughout the study as a whole.

3 This is the service obtained by a cable subscriber paying the minimum charge. It will normally comprise the broadcast services plus a range of other 'free' channels. A 'basic channel' is one included in the basic service.

4 Sometimes called a 'subscription channel', this is available only for additional subscription over and above the basic service.

5 In a few areas, AsiaVision was available only as a subscription channel, probably further defining its viewership by ethnic origin.

6 This is a derogatory descriptor for a 'black' (used in its wider sense to refer to peoples of African-Caribbean and Asian Origin) person who is perceived as acting like, or exhibiting behavioural characteristics more commonly associated with, a white person. The image approximates to the description of the coconut fruit: black on the outside, white on the inside. The most obvious line of attack is if a black person speaks in 'too English' in accent.

13   Identity TV

Patrick Ismond

Background information

At the time of my PhD research, the relatively new African-Caribbean oriented cable station *Identity* TV (IDTV) was also based and operated in London. In 1993, it was installed on three of the major cable systems and covered the whole of the capital. Then, IDTV hoped to expand outside London, to areas where African-Caribbean residents were most densely populated, before becoming a nationwide cable service. According to IDTV/BET's opening press release, their longer-term aims were consistent with this expansion, as the station hoped to transmit via satellite and become available in Europe. The ITC Annual Report indicated that 160,000 homes had access to IDTV, as part of their *basic* package of cable channels (ITC, 1993).

IDTV is in partnership with *Black Entertainment Television* (BET). BET was founded in 1980 as an African-American focused entertainment service on US network TV. It is itself backed by two major US corporate investors - Telecommunications Inc. and Home Box Office. BET's primary role is to provide a predominantly entertainment service for the African-American consumer, another fact made clear by its opening press release:

[BET's] programming line-up features...music videos, news and public affairs, jazz, specials, off-network sitcoms, gospel and college sports programmes.

Since 1992, BET has also been operating on satellite, 24 hours a day. In line with commercial trends of acquisitions and mergers in the industry, it has cross-subsidised its audio-visual operation by marketing products; through diversifying into 'youth' magazine publishing; and through co-ownership of a film production company.

Aims, access and the cultural politics of representation

What are the programme aims of an African-Caribbean-oriented cable TV service? The channel's Co-Director indicated that addressing issues of cultural identity was a prime factor to be reflected in programming content. In her words:

> The dictionary definition for 'identity' is 'individual characteristics which one is easily recognised by'. So therefore our channel, once you tune into us, I guess the identity on it is obviously a black identity, which is very important to our people, and therefore an appropriate name for it.

The prominence assigned to debates around the construction of black identities is evinced by a growing body of literature in this area (see for example Gilroy, 1993a, b). In a media context, a debate about the foci for black cultural production explores key areas of the interplay between culture and identity (see for example Hussein, 1994; Ismond, 1994).

Before her association with IDTV, the Co-Director compiled a questionnaire to 'evaluate black people's television viewing habits and tastes'. The results confirmed her own thinking in this area and are interlinked with her conception of the role of the channel. The Co-Director claimed that:

> [The reason why] we started this was that we weren't having enough images, black images, on television in general, in all the different types of areas that one might see their white counterparts. So in a way Identity [the cable station] is mixed up in that. It's exposure of your identity in a medium that is readily recognised.

A debate about the 'quality' and 'quantity' of black media images reveals the extent to which these perspectives are seen as 'oppositional'. The essence of this debate is 'timing': at what point is there an extensive enough repertoire of black images such that the more stereotypical ones are interpreted as dramatic pretence, rather than defining black social reality? (MacDonald, 1992).

IDTV's publicity brochure places an emphasis on programming high 'quality', that is 'specifically acquired with [the] target audience in mind'. It is also seen as important for the programmes to be distinctively different from any (mainstream) offerings targeted towards black people, and therefore to fill gaps left in the broadcast schedules by existing TV programmes. This conception of the role of 'minority' broadcasting is a key element of the debate concerning which system provides the best basis for media democratisation. The 'choice' is generally presented in terms of binary opposites: either a system which caters more adequately for a plurality of interests, or one which abrogates broader responsibility for less commercial interests to the cornucopia of 'dedicated' channels.

Did the channel's programming cater for differentiation *within* the black audience, by social class, gender and age? The Co-Director felt that:

> These sorts of questions can only really be justified, quantified by research. The way our programming is structured is that we're on air 18 hours a day in any

case. We package up to six-hour blocks of programming. We start at 12 noon till 6 pm. So we know that we obviously cover the people who are at home during the day with kids, you know, mums or whatever. Then we repeat that from 6 pm till midnight, so obviously the people who have worked during the day will obviously see it. Then midnight to 6 am, so obviously once again we capture that sort of market-getting people who are probably nightworkers or something. Class...is a difficult issue. Music transcends class. Obviously a lot of our product is music-orientated so we think that, not only on the music side, a lot of our music transcends class and race. The channel we know is targeted to the Afro-Caribbeans, but it's not exclusive to the Afro-Caribbeans. We know that, from the calls we get anyway into the office, that the channel is received very well by our Caucasian counterparts, our Asian counterparts. So it's not an exclusively black channel for black people. We know we've got a lot more to offer others as well.

A typical programming template for the rolling schedule reads as follows:

12:00-18:00, 18:00-24:00, 24:00-06:00

♦ A documentary from the Caribbean;
♦ an interview with an African-American academic, intellectual or other person, or a West Indian comedy;
♦ a music show. Currently, the popular *Video Soul* show;
♦ a soap or drama. It is seen as important that these are transmitted during 'prime-time', to compete with the broadcast soaps such as *Coronation Street* and *Eastenders*;
♦ a jazz music show;
♦ a rap music show.

The logic behind IDTV, therefore, appears not to be as 'ethnically-specific' as that of AsiaVision. There is no explicit assumption about the work patterns of particular class members within the African-Caribbean target audience, or the propensity of female audiences to watch certain programme genres. The template shows that music predominates as the form of entertainment on the network, confirming its cheapness and accessibility to general viewing audiences. Its prominence also appears to indicate that music is the greatest concession to diversity within the black audience offered by the channel. Significantly, the large proportion of American music on the channel raises issues around the construction of black, *British* identities, further discussed below.

Also, the bulk of the new channel's programming was imported. African and Caribbean programming comprised a part of this import, but under the terms of their agreement with BET, the latter provided IDTV with a significant proportion of its programmes. An analysis of the schedule, at the time of research, revealed that, on average, some four-and-a-half to five hours of programming in any one day (six-hour schedule) were imported from BET's programme library. Notwithstanding, the Co-Director claimed that:

> [Although] the bulk of our channel is imported product...we do have three UK main strands. We've got a UK reggae show which goes into the clubs off London areas. We'll get acts from these which are interspersed with music and video and so on. We also have an African magazine show which is on a biweekly basis at the moment which looks at what's happening in Africa but from a UK bias. And we also have what I would term as an '01 for London'-type show which is a fast-moving news, information and entertainment-type show which is once again in and around London, what's happening. Our goal in a way is to reduce our foreign product and upgrade our UK product so that, in fact, the UK product at some point can dominate. But the industry that we're in at the moment means that we just cannot saw through the

UK in the strength that we would like. That's the difficulty.

This 'UK product' seems to depart from the music diet typical of the channel as a whole. It is characteristic of the 'infotainment'-type programming that is becoming increasingly popular on mainstream TV and is relatively cheap to produce. However, the predominance of BET programming on the channel reflects the cost difference between producing, and transmitting already-produced, 'popular' programming. As we have seen in relation to AsiaVision, the same cost forces that make it cheaper to provide a diet of music, in this instance, also signal a low level of investment in black, British-made products. This point was made clear by the Co-Director, who attempted to explain this by pointing to changes in the industry as a whole, rather than an absence of will on her organisation's part:

> At the moment I don't think it's going to be difficult for us to encourage our people to write scripts. I mean I've got I think two in my in-tray so far without any prompting. What I've found is that there is no question that we are fully talented in that area. It's just a question once again of...in a way, creating the right medium, which we have...but once again funding, money...because a lot of these projects need a lot of money to do it. Not a lot sometimes, but you need enough to sustain the thing right the way through. And it's not for the lack of projects, and it's not for the lack of talent and it's not for the lack of scripts...It's in a way talk about infrastructures. It's the industry that we find ourselves in. The infrastructure is so weak. There's no encouragement generally. There's no film industry so, you know, the film industry usually spins off the TV industry and so on. No, there's nothing there really...At the moment, we made it very clear that we're not commissioning any products because we don't yet have the funds to

underwrite that sort of scheme. From the interest we've generated so far, we're going to have to implement one [a commissioning structure] as time goes on. But we're a new start-up, we're a young company. We know the direction in which we have to go and it's possibly along the commissioning route.

In view of the cost pressures that have resulted in constraints on domestic production, it is quite likely that the proportions of BET programming for the channel will continue at present levels, or indeed rise. If BET were to provide IDTV with a reduced volume of programming, it would stand to lose a potentially lucrative showcase. In the longer term, an arrangement whereby BET leases more technical equipment to IDTV cannot compare with the potential return on investment in 'popular' programming.

Additionally, a US-dominated programme schedule raises key concerns around the construction of distinct black, *British* identities. Taylor (1994) has celebrated the career achievements and cultural mores of 'Afro-Saxons', a specific black, British identity. On the other hand, Gilroy (1993a, 1993b) has noted that the promotion and commercial dissemination of African-American cultural products has led to their 'authentication' as universal statements on black identity, thereby overlooking and negating conceptions of British blackness. In the current, US-dominated internationalised climate, the latter assertion has assumed more prominence.

The discouragement of home-grown independent production demonstrates that cable's potential role in the media's democratisation is currently largely unfulfilled. It is arguable that cable has been promoted in idealised terms: a way of visualising the possible rather than describing reality (see for example Hollins, 1984). In its present state, a number of interventions would be needed to offset the brute force of commercialism which increasingly defines media organisation and output as a whole (see for example Williams, 1994). In this light, the Co-Director's comments on the media's future role in the lives of Britain's black population appear strikingly optimistic; they perhaps illustrate a future conception of the media where commercial forces are less intractable and deterministic than at present. They appear to endorse the view that, in an increasingly fragmented market, acquiring and keeping smaller niche markets will assume greater importance to advertisers and programmers, and will be reflected in programming content. The Co-Director stated that:

> I think it [the media] hasn't been important in the past...I think it's going to be extremely important in the future...TV is people's main leisure time. I think it's going to play a more important role and, dare I say it, with the existence of Identity Television people are going to realise that, 'Hey, there is something for us, you know, targeted, tailor-made for us. Let's use it.' Because we know that television as a medium is a very powerful medium. So I think in our day-to-day lives, it's going to become more important than we know. With television we're going to be able to...do our banking over the phone et cetera...it will be more important than ever.

Controls, constraints and limitations

What are the controls and constraints identified by the cable operator IDTV working in the independent commercial sector? Again, it is useful to start, as per AsiaVision earlier, with the personal thoughts about racism as a constraint in the media industry. Asia Vision's MD gave some indication of the existence of institutionalised racism as reflected in social organisations and structures. As a black person with work experience at the BBC, Identity's Co-Director suggested that black media professionals working there have to adapt if they want to survive, or have a particular 'mind-set' to start with - an interesting observation in the light of the earlier claims of BBC producers:

> Most of our talented black media people are going to

'cut their teeth', whether they like it or not, in main-stream television: BBC, the ITVs. They're going to come up through those ranks. And I think...although the BBC and ITV have gone to great lengths to promote...the recruitment of black and Asian people into the media...without a doubt, those individuals who are recruited in that way will be under no illusion that it is a very difficult place to be in as a black individual, in mainstream TV...The BBC is a very 'constrained' place...in that they have their own model, and if you fall outside of that model...things become a little difficult...They would never say 'black this' or 'black that' to your face but by nature of the BBC, it's very Oxford and Cambridge...and you'll clash upon management at some point...Yes, I think that there is underlying racism, probably not up front. (Co-Director)

The Co-Director's comments lend weight to charges, detailed in relation to AsiaVision, that minority media personnel are invariably 'co-opted and contained' by the dominant value system: one in which it is difficult to redefine minority ethnic agendas. Her comments also indicate that the ground appears to have shifted from a concern with the 'quantity', or numbers, of minority ethnic person-nel working in the mainstream media. Instead, the Co-Director conveys a sense that minority ethnic commitment, and the capacity to challenge institutional structures from within, are primary consid-erations. Certainly, minority ethnic recruitment to the BBC and ITV companies is a stated aim. Nonetheless, statistics indicate that their employment is skewed towards the lower grades on the one hand whilst, conversely, being offset by cosmetic changes in an increas-ing number of black faces in front of the camera (see ITC, 1993; BBC, 1992; Downing and Husband, 1994). We could also consider whether minority ethnic perceptions of the industry, with its nega-tion of concerns around issues of culture and identity, would dis-courage access *before* the point of entry.

At any rate, the Co-Director's view is endorsed by the findings of a small-scale research project involving interviews with former minority ethnic employees of the mainstream media. The responses highlighted the media's capacity to stifle attempts at expressing cultural identities outside of a narrowly-defined ethnic compass (see Ismond, 1994).

In contrast to findings noted in the case study of AsiaVision, the Co-Director felt that the relationship between advertisers and minority ethnic media outlets was evolving into a positive one:

> Research so far into the cable viewer shows that we do hit the ABC1s...and even the C2s or whatever they call them...For a company that is so young as ours, we are picking up corporate advertisers. I think printed media is very different from television media. Television is the number one leisure time people have...In a way, advertisers will probably see us along the same lines...we're a minority media, but they know also that minority media sells. And I think...the realisation is dawning that Afro-Caribbeans are like all black people in this country. They like to be catered for, and they like things to be tailor-made for them. The climate whereby advertisers, sponsors...could tag an advert underneath *Desmonds* [a black comedy show on television] and expect to sell it to black homes is changing rapidly...Black people are now realising that we have to patronise our own in a big way. Instead of going to a MacDonald's, we'll probably go to a Caribbean take-away...and you know they're always well patronised... That is the tide of change, if you like. (Co-Director)

The Co-Director's comments again endorse the view that fragmented consumer markets will assume increasing importance to advertisers, particularly to counter a drift towards minority-owned businesses. Presumably, this 'tide of change' also encompasses a commitment to viewing the channel!

Although high programme prices were seen as a constraint for the channel, commercial necessity seems to have generated its own compromise solution, as it is in the interest of the programme supplier, the cable station and advertisers to secure some sort of agreement. The Co-Director stated that:

> There already is a product that we should be buying that we cannot buy...films, particularly movies with strong black leads, quality black products...The price would probably be prohibitive for us at this time. But...we've managed to find products at the price we can afford to pay...There are sources you can tap for programming at a price that you can meet. So in a way, pricing for programming is always negotiable, and it's always flexible.

There is little doubt that securing 'high quality' programming is crucial to retain viewer loyalty and commitment to the channel. Perhaps a more contentious issue concerns the pressure for 'political' compromise attendant on some funding sources in relation to the content of programming. Nonetheless, the Co-Director claimed that:

> I don't see funding sources as an issue. Politically, I don't think there's a tie-in with your funding to your political voice. This channel will always in a way be self-financing, we hope....At the moment, we haven't been reliant on anyone except our backers [BET]...who are a like-for-like [service]...We are not constrained by a backer or by a provider of funds....who is basically pulling our strings or basically giving us a political complexion that we don't want.

The fact that the channel is entertainment-oriented may lessen the possibility of such an ideological clash. With the possible exception of some dramas and forms of music, these genres are arguably unsuited as a regular platform for socio-political debate (see for example Barry, 1988).

Competition *between* the cable stations in these case studies is predominantly for advertising revenue, reflecting very real differences in the minority ethnic cultures of AsiaNet and IDTV's respective target audiences. As a music-based entertainment channel, IDTV also sees itself competing with satellite's *MTV* and with *Channel Four* for viewers and advertising revenue.

Summary

Identity TV is an entertainment service that relies heavily on a diet of music and relatively cheap, magazine-type 'infotainment' programming that is also 'popular' and easy to produce. American dominance is reflected in large contributions not only to the music schedule, but also to other imported material (dramas, soaps, films) on the channel. In opting for the degree of commercial safety that musical and other popular formats bring, a number of issues are raised which are germane to this study.

The channel's declared aim to explore constructions of black cultural identities is difficult to discern in a British context, given its programming diet and reliance on imports. In this vein, music appears to be the greatest concession to differences within the black audience. The global dissemination of black American music has significantly defined the debate on black identity, in a way that perhaps leaves little room for the construction of black Britishness. It would seem that commercial forces are moulding the content of IDTV away from the narrowcasting potential promoted as a social fillip to cable's development and expressed in the contributions of local talent. One of the consequences of low-level investment in domestic production is that it does not augur well for the promotion of cable as a showcase for innovative and experimental (read 'risky') material.

Further, institutionalised racism, reflected in social organisations and structures, was seen to act as a blockage to black media access, in line with findings for AsiaVision. At a more structural level, high programme costs operated against the channel's preferred schedule but, unlike the experience of AsiaVision, programme prices were negotiable. In view of their entertainment focus, the content of these same programmes proved not to be a funding issue in the way that it did for AsiaNet. Competition for advertising revenue lay predominantly with other *music* broadcasters, defining the commonly-perceived character of the channel.

Conclusion

This study has examined the programming aims, cultural and political concerns, and financial problems confronting cable operators servicing minority ethnic groups in the commercial sector. A common denominator influencing these issues for the two cable channels is the negative relationship between programming and finance, whether advertising or subscription. More specifically, a deregulated commercial market appears to have a number of important consequences for the channel's operation, and therefore this study. Firstly, it is orienting the general product towards forms of entertainment which are cheap to buy and have a broad-based, rather than specific-interest, appeal. Second and conversely, it is at best limiting, and at worst excluding controversial, political programming, principally the *documentary* and *current affairs* genres. Thirdly, the market appears to discourage the fulfilment of cable's narrowcasting role, which would partly be manifested in the channel's use as a showcase for local media and production talent.

Whether market forces especially constrain the operation of minority ethnic media is an important issue, and the struggle to obtain advertising revenue proves instructive. Personnel involved in minority ethnic media claim that it is difficult to convince the more established advertisers that black people can deliver an attractive and (in some ways) different audience in sufficient numbers. There is also a perceived problem of ensuring that the right price will be secured to enable big-name clients to sell their products (Phillips-Eteng, 1988). More recently, Saad Ali, a media analyst specialising in minority ethnic markets stated: 'ignorance is the biggest problem. Advertisers don't know about ethnic communities and what you don't know you don't touch' (cited in Syedain, 1993, p. 38). A comparison of the fortunes of the major commercial stations with minority ethnic media may yield some answers.

Although their conceptions of the role of the media in the lives of minority ethnic audiences may differ, the cable operators share a desire (along with the producers of Cottle's study) for their programming to provide an alternative and 'richer vision' (Husband, 1994) to present televisual reality: improved representation of minority ethnic agendas and experiences. Cottle's research has also highlighted the independent's scramble for scarce revenue from various sources. Their experiences were analogous to those of the cable operators although, in the case of AsiaNet, there was the more pronounced dimension of trying to get unconditional funding.

It is likely that the future of cable narrowcasting for minority ethnic groups will very much hinge on the confluence of forces shaping its present. For this reason, minority ethnic media will need a greater degree of 'self stability'. This could take the form of more donations from black businesses and organisations, as well as government mandatory grants. This help would enable cable to attend more fully to the plurality of identities within the 'African Caribbean' and 'Asian' labels, as well as providing an infrastructure for the commissioning of work from the local community. As it stands, the alternative appears to lie in the direction of programming that AsiaVision's Managing Director aptly classified as 'Sky Television with a black face': cheap, commercial programming that is distinguishable from its mainstream counterpart only in the ethnic identity of the presenters and other personnel involved.

In light of the above, it is significant that a recent press report on IDTV (Cumberbatch, June 25, 1996), has asked questions of its programme content. The channel has now opted for an exclusively

207

musical (jazz) format and the commercial safety that promises, as a result of 'a combination of poor programming and a lack of advertising' (Cumberbatch, ibid, p.7). In so doing, the channel has moved further away from its original remit, of fulfilling cable's narrowcasting role, and has endorsed the less welcome findings of this study regarding the difficulties attendant on servicing minority ethnic audiences in the commercial sector.

Part Four
Conclusion

14   Conclusion

This study has attended to the aims and experiences, concerns and problems of producers and how these influence the production of minority ethnic television programmes. Both 'insider' accounts of in-house producers working at the BBC and those working 'outside' in the independent sector have been considered, as well as those of cable TVprofessionals 'circling the fence'of terrestrial broadcasting. Experienced and established, aspiring and emergent, commercially oriented and politically committed producers have all been consulted. What they generally share, however, is commitment to make television programmes that in some way provide enhanced representations of minority ethnic experiences, agendas of concern and value positions. Collectively they work in an increasingly competitive and commercialised environment, whether inside the BBC or outside it in the independent and cable sectors, and they must negotiate a cultural-political stance in relation to the shifting sands of ethnic identity and politics of 'race'. Often they confront similar problems, whether difficulties of securing sufficient finance, dealing with institutional gatekeepers and commissioners or steering a course between contending political positions and audience expectations. These and other formidable problems confronting producers of ethnic minority programmes have been identified and discussed across the study.

Important differences also obtain. Typically differentiating the commercial independent production companies from those small-scale, local and community-based organisations are organisational aims and positions on the cultural politics of representation. Not that political distinctions necessarily fall neatly into place according to whether funding is commercial or grant-aided; most of the independents consulted now feel obliged, notwithstanding the cultural costs, to seek out sources of commercial support to supplement a patchwork quilt of small grants, subsidies and other sources of funding. Established mainstream producers continue to hold on, albeit by their finger-nails, to earlier ideas of 'intervening' into the mainstream with programmes that resonate with ideas and experiences from the varied minority ethnic communities and perspectives. Working in close proximity with the major television institutions, which are themselves constrained to function in an increasingly commercial, competitive and deregulated environment, the producers' degree of independence and creative latitude has apparently become curtailed. Though also experiencing difficulties of funding, small-scale community-based independents are often informed by more expressly political agendas and representational commitments. This too is further differentiated in terms of the politics pursued, with one stance apparently seeking to dislodge and counter dominant stereotypes with more 'truthful' and 'accurate' representations, while another seeks to shake off any notion of a singular representational mission on behalf of *the* black community, and to creatively explore diverse images and forms that resonate with the changing conditions, experiences and identities of complexly constituted black audiences.

In-house BBC producers, for their part, have helped provide a rare insiders' view into the professional and production environment of multicultural programmes made within the heartland of British public service broadcasting. A less than positive picture of the BBC was painted. Notwithstanding the BBC's public commitment to equal opportunities, notwithstanding a plethora of training and other schemes designed to increase minority ethnic involvement within

212

the Corporation, as well as its declared statements of intent relating to both mainstream and special or targeted programmes for ethnic minorities, the producers recounted a relatively staid and unadventurous, hierarchical and bureaucratically remote, production ethos and environment - an ethos and environment that apparently inhibits and constrains the aims and creative expression of many of its programme makers. The producers themselves, however, are also implicated in maintaining BBC traditions of programme making in so far as many of them appear to have adopted the mantle of BBC 'professionalism' - a programme-making stance emphasising political neutrality and the production of programmes high in production values for the 'mainstream'. A stance, in other words, professionally disinclined to champion the production of politically engaged and innovative programmes, some of which at least should be directed solely at ethnic minority audiences. Working in the pressurised and competitive environment of the BBC, and seeking a claim to equal professional status in relation to colleagues working in other BBC departments, such a response may be pragmatic and understandable, but the consequences for the production of ethnic minority programmes are nonetheless tangible. An index of the producers' disenchantment with the BBC is found in their expressed concerns about the future of ethnic minority programme production. Despite recent public statements of intent committing the Corporation to continued production of ethnic minority programmes, the producers tended to see a different future scenario. They questioned how long special programme departments will be able to continue at the BBC, an institution that is surrounded by, and increasingly responsive to, the competitive and market-driven communications environment.

The study of two Cable TV operators narrowcasting to distinct ethnic minorities has also demonstrated the powerful constraining effects of the marketplace. Notwithstanding the widespread hopes placed in cable as a force for enhanced minority ethnic representation, local involvement and democratic advance, Patrick Ismond's study arrived at an opposite conclusion. The forces of a deregulated marketplace are thought to have resulted in the following: increased transmission of cheap entertainment imports; marginalisation, if not exclusion, of current affairs and documentary genres - programme forms central to serious political television; and also the relegation of its hoped-for showcase role in which local talent, production experience and expertise could be developed.

Across the different sectors of the television industry, the production of ethnic minority programmes is thus shaped and constrained by powerful forces. The institutional and regulatory frameworks now structuring the television industry do not appear to be conducive to the development of enhanced ethnic minority representation. The BBC works within an increasingly competitive landscape, is expected to justify its licence fee, and seeks to do this by producing programmes with wide appeal. ITV is fiercely competitive and commercially driven - advertising sales and audience ratings are the name of the game here, with programmes bought or produced for the largest possible audiences. Soon to be joined by Channel Five, the competitive environment is poised to be given a further twist. Channel Four, once the hope of minority programming, appears to have moved away from its original remit, as the innovatory break between direct advertising sales and programme commissioning/ transmission is once again bridged. Though the Broadcasting Act, 1990, still requires Channel Four to 'appeal to tastes and interests not generally catered for by ITV' and 'encourage innovation and experiment', it is apparent that the schedules in relation to ethnic minority programmes include increasing numbers of imported soaps and entertainment genres. The requirement placed on all major broadcasters by the Broadcasting Act, 1990, to commission at least 25 percent of their original programme output from independent production companies has not resulted in breaking the established monopolies of programme production. If anything, the move appears to have accelerated the process of commercial consolidation of a few major production companies which now dominate the marketplace. Small-scale production companies and emergent producers interested in producing programming for ethnic minority audiences find precious few opportunities to compete and gain a foothold in the field of established networks and commissioner-producer contacts. Given the precarious dependency of producers on commissioners, the latter can exert a decisive influence upon proposed programme ideas, and in any case increasingly commission on the basis of pre-determined schedule slots 'requiring' certain types of programmes.

Producers must work within these constraints if they want to produce programmes for the major television outlets; cable TV narrowcasting, as we have heard, is perhaps even more exposed to the pressures and constraints of the marketplace. At a time when creative opportunities appear to be more tightly controlled than ever, it is perhaps worth considering the continuing value of special programme provision. Critics of so-called 'ghetto programmes' have long questioned the strategic value of separate departments, arguing that these simply appease institutional consciences and permit continuing complacency across the range of other programme departments. They act, in other words, as a break upon the successful entry of minority ethnic producers into the television industry more generally, and also inhibit the production of challenging minority ethnic programmes produced for mainstream audiences. The television industry is fast changing, however. The idea that any single strategy to effect change and enhance representation would have a monopoly of impact seems improbable. The television industry is structured across the public and private sectors in complex ways, ways that will become, courtesy of new information and communication technologies, increasingly complex and fragmented in the future.

If the television industry and new technologies are set to fragment audiences, the changing politics of identity also looks set to continue to fragment audiences ideologically and culturally. As ideas about fixed ethnic identities become challenged both theoretically and experientially when witnessing or participating in the fluid, multiple and overlapping cultural expressions of social difference, so ideas of ethnic minority representation are rendered increasingly problematic. If some of the black film-makers of the 1980s grappled with these difficult questions at the level of subject matter, narrative and form, and helped galvanise serious theoretical debates and discussion both then and subsequently, this moment does not appear to

215

have informed the practice of television producers and would-be producers working in the middle to late 1990s. Though a general position is shared by the producers who argue for the necessity of a dual approach to 'representation', involving the deliberate pursuit of increased training opportunities and access to the television industry behind the screen, as well as access and enhanced representations on screen, they are constrained by the limited funding opportunities and scheduling needs of major television institutions competing within an increasingly deregulated marketplace. Considerations of form, as we have heard, now very much equate with the increased use of popular and populist formats. Concepts such as cultural 'hybridity', 'cultural syncretism' and 'translation' help draw attention to the dynamic fusion and interplay between different cultural forces and identities. In terms of the current configuration of the television industry and its programme orientations, questions of cultural fusion and interplay are likely, however, to be reduced to those of the latest infotainment format.

At the outset of the study, producers were said to be positioned between the forces of the marketplace, regulation and new technologies on the one side, and the contested and changing cultural politics of 'race' and ethnicity on the other. The testimonies of the producers have provided ample support to this view, where both sets of forces have been found to impact upon and are played out in institutional and production settings. How these forces interact and shape the active programme making processes, from design to production to transmission, has only just begun to be examined however. This study has only scratched the surface of the complexities and difficulties involved, though hopefully some of the major forces at work - professional, ideological, institutional and structural - have been mapped. There is clearly need for further research and improved information.

The study has noted the surprising lack of available information and systematic monitoring of ethnic minority involvement within and across the television industry. Public declarations of commitment to equal opportunities by major television institutions are difficult to reconcile with the paucity of, and often hopelessly blunt, data known and/or made available by them - a finding criticised on a number of occasions throughout the study. The concept of 'ethnic minority' may indeed pose problems of classification, while the dynamic nature of television production and organisation does not permit easy monitoring and quantification. That said, the television industry has a particular responsibility to 'represent' wider society, both on screen and behind it in the workplace. Only with systematic monitoring and the generation of accurate and detailed information can this fundamental aim be put into practice within the production context; and only then can public pronouncements of intent, whether from the BBC, Channel Four or other corporate television players, be taken seriously. It is in the nature of television to 'represent'; it must be challenged to become more 'representative' and publicly accountable. The study has also demonstrated the need for further research.

A more detailed and retrospective study of the changing experiences and fortunes of established independents commissioned by the BBC would put flesh on the bones of historical change as experienced by the producers themselves. Their relationship to, and possible changing stance towards, the cultural politics of representation deserve detailed study, perhaps with a more focused approach to the differences, possibilities and changing nature of television genres.

The changing organisational forms and cultural-political aims of community-based independents and independent production companies also demand detailed historical and comprehensive research. This study has managed to consult only some of the many organisations currently operative; a more comprehensive survey would certainly provide information for a refined understanding of the companies and organisations operating in what is now a fast-changing field. Here the method most likely to reveal something of the cultural depth and complexities involved is participant-observation; ethnography alone is capable of supplementing interview findings with insights into the working practices and cultural ethos informing production-based activities. It can observe processes of economic and cultural *mediation* as they are played out in professional

217

programme-making activities - processes that are not always consciously pursued or fully articulated in an interview situation.

Similarly, if issues of access could be resolved, special programme departments *and* mainstream departments within the BBC, and other major television institutions, demand intensive fieldwork study, including the observation of programme commissioning, design, production and post-production activity. Only with intense research such as this can a more detailed picture of the nuances and differences of organisational approach, professional ideology and cultural engagement be understood and mapped in relation to those overarching contexts of historical, institutional and cultural-political change - an approach also likely to prove productive if applied to cable TV operations and other minority focused communication technologies.

Television producers, it was suggested at the outset, have always tended to be invested with too much explanatory significance by television commentators, and yet rarely have they been subject to the detailed consideration that often accompanies their programmes. As this study has illustrated, the producers work within, and constantly negotiate their way through, a force-field of constraints, influences and changing conditions. Only with detailed empirical analysis will we be able to fully identify and comprehend the extent and influence of these changing conditions upon producer practices and their programme representations. If this task is of continuing relevance to the television production scene, in the present broadcasting conjuncture it has added urgency in relation to concerns of minority ethnic television production.

References

Alibhai-Brown, Y. (1994) 'Sold Out by Media Wallahs', *New Statesman and Society*, January 28, pp.34-35.

Anwar, M. and Shang, A. (1982) *Television in a Multi-racial Society: A Research Report*, London: Commission for Racial Equality.

Asia Net (1993) *AsiaNet: The US/Indian and Pakistani Connection*, Asia Net Publicity Pack.

Barry, A. (1988) 'Black Mythologies: Representation of Black People on British Television', in J. Twitchin (ed.) *The Black and White Media Show Book*, Stoke on Trent: Trentham Books, pp.83-102.

BBC (1992) *Annual Report 1991/92*, London: BBC.

BBC (1993) *Producer Choice*, London: BBC.

BBC (1995a) *People and Programmes*, London: BBC.

BBC (1995b) *1994/95 Report and Accounts,* London: BBC.

BBC (1995c) 'BBC Plans New Approach for Multicultural Programmes' *News Release*, BBC Press Office, September, BBC Pebble Mill, Birmingham.

Butterworth, E. (1967) 'The 1962 Smallpox Outbreak and the British Press', *Race,* 7(4): 347-64.

Bygrave, M. (1994) 'Movement of the People', *The Guardian*

Weekend, August 20, pp.28-33.

Cabinet Office, Information Technology Advisory Panel (1982) *Report on Cable Systems*, London: HMSO.

Chan, J.M. (1994) 'National Responses and Accessibility of STAR TV in Asia', *Journal of Communications*, Summer, 44(3): 112-131.

Channel Four (1996) *Report and Financial Statements* 1995, London: Channel Four.

Church, L.M. (1987) 'Community Access Television: What We Don't Know and Why We Don't Know It', *Journal of Film and Video*, 39(3): 6-13.

Corner, J., Harvey, S. and Lury, K. (1994) 'Culture, Quality and Choice: The Re-regulation of TV 1989-91' in S. Hood (ed.) *Behind the Screens: The Structure of British Television in the Nineties*, London: Lawrence and Wishart.

Cottle, S. (1992) "Race", Racialization and the Media: A Review and Update of Research', *Sage Race Relations Abstracts*, 17(2): 3-57.

Cottle, S. (1993a) *TV News, Urban Conflict and the Inner City*, Leicester: Leicester University Press.

Cottle, S. (1993b) '"Race" and Regional Television News: Multi-culturalism and the Production of Popular TV' *New Community*, 19(4): 581-592.

Cottle, S. (1993c) 'Behind the Headlines: The Sociology of News', pp. 478-492 in M. O'Donnell (ed.) *New Introductory Readings in Sociology*, Walton-on-Thames: Thomas Nelson.

Cottle, S. (1994a) 'The News Media and "Race" - A Case of Intended and Unintended Outcomes', *Social Science Teacher*, 23(2): 12-14.

Cottle, S. (1994b) 'Stigmatizing Handsworth: Notes on Reporting Spoiled Space', *Critical Studies in Mass Communication*, 11(3): 231-256.

Cottle, S. (1995a) 'Producer-Driven Television?', Review Essay, *Media Culture and Society*, 17(1): 169-176.

Cottle, S. (1995b) 'The Production of News Formats: Determinants of Mediated Contestation', *Media, Culture and Society*, 17(2):

275-291.

Cottle, S. (1996) 'Analysing Still and Moving Images' Module Five: Unit 30, pp.213-242. MA Distance Learning, Centre for Mass Communication Research, University of Leicester.

Cottle, S. (1997) 'Participant Observation: Researching News Production', in A. Hansen, S. Cottle, R. Negrine, C. Newbold *Mass Communication Research Methods*, London: Macmillan.

Crisell, A. (1992) *Understanding Radio*, London: Methuen.

Critcher, C., Parker, M. and Sondhi, R. (1977) *Race in the Provincial Press*, Paris: UNESCO.

Cumberbatch, S. (1996) 'Pulling the Plug and all that Jazz', *The Voice*, June 25, p.7.

Daniels, T. (1990) 'Beyond Negative or Positive Images', in J.Willis and T. Wollen (eds.) *The Neglected Audience*, London: British Film Institute, pp.66-71.

Daniels, T. (1994) 'Programmes For Black Audiences' in S. Hood (ed.) *Behind The Screens: The Structure of British Television in the Nineties*, London: Lawrence and Wishart.

Daniels, T. and Gerson, J. (eds.) (1989) *The Colour Black: Black Images in British Television*, London: British Film Institute Publishing.

Dhondy, F. (1992) 'Farrukh Dhondy' Interview in J. Pines (ed.) *Black and White in Colour*, London: British Film Institute Publishing.

Docherty, D., Morrison, D. E. and Tracey, M. (1988) *Keeping Faith?: Channel Four and its Audience*, London: John Libbey.

Downing, J. and Husband, C. (1994) 'Media Flows, Ethnicity, Racism and Xenophobia', a paper presented at the *Media Flows Research Symposium*, University of Tampere, September 3-6.

Elliott, P. (1972) *The Making of a Television Series*, London: Constable.

Fenton, S. (1996) 'Counting Ethnicity: Social Groups and Official Catergories' in R. Levitas and W. Guy (eds) *Interpreting Official Statistics*, London: Routledge

Fuller, L. (1993), *Community Television in the United States*, New York: Greenwood Press.

Gillespie, M. (1995) *Television, Ethnicity and Cultural Change*, London: Routledge.

Gilroy, P. (1993a), *The Black Atlantic*, London: Verso.

Gilroy, P. (1993b), *Small Acts*, London: Serpents Tail.

Givanni, J. (ed.) (1995) *Remote Control,* London: British Film Institute.

Gordon, P. (1990), *Racial Violence and Harassment*, London: Runnymede Trust.

Gordon, P. and Rosenberg, D. (1989) *Daily Racism - The Press and Black People in Britain,* London: The Runnymede Trust.

Gray, H. (1995) *Watching Race: Television and the Struggle for 'Blackness'*, Minneapolis/London: University of Minnesota Press.

Hall, S. (1988) 'New Ethnicities' in K. Mercer (ed.) *Black Film, British Cinema*, ICA Documents 7. London: British Film Institute, pp.27-31.

Hall, S. (1990) 'The Whites of their Eyes: Racist Ideologies and the Media' in M. Alvarado and J.O. Thompson (eds.), *The Media Reader*, London: British Film Institute, pp.8-23.

Hall, S. (1992), 'What is this "Black" in Black Popular Culture?', in G. Dent (ed.), *Black Popular Culture*, Seattle: Bay Press, pp.21-36.

Hall, S. (1995) 'Black and White in Television' in J. Givanni (ed.) *Remote Control,* London: British Film Institute.

Hall, S., Chritcher, C., Jefferson, T., Clarke, J. and Roberts, B. (1978) *Policing the Crisis: Mugging, The State, and Law and Order*, Basingstoke: Macmillan.

Halloran, J. (1974) 'Mass Media and Race: A Research Approach' in UNESCO (ed.), *Race As News*, Paris: UNESCO.

Halloran, J.D., Bhatt, A. and Gray. P. (1995) *Ethnic Minorities and Television: A Study of Use, Reactions and Preferences*, Leicester: Centre for Mass Communication Research, University of Leicester.

Hansen, A. and Murdock, G. (1985) 'Constructing the Crowd: Populist Discourse and Press Presentation' in V. Mosco and M. Wasco (eds.), *Popular Culture and Media Events,* The Critical

Communication Review. Vol. III, New Jersey: Ablex, pp.227-57.

Hartmann, P. and Husband, C. (1974) *Racism and the Mass Media*, London: Davis Poynter.

Hartmann, P., Husband. C. and Clark, J. (1974) 'Race as News: A Study in the Handling of Race in the British Press from 1963 to 1970' in UNESCO (ed.), *Race as News*, Paris: UNESCO.

Harvey, S. (1994) 'Channel 4 Television: From Annan to Grade' in S. Hood (ed.), *Behind the Screens: The Structure of British Television in the Nineties*, London: Lawrence and Wishart.

Holland, P. (1981) 'The New Cross Fire and the Popular Press' *Multi-Racial Education*, 9(3): 61-80.

Hollins, T. (1984), *Beyond Broadcasting: Into the Cable Age*, London: British Film Institute.

Hood, S. (ed.) (1994) *Behind the Screens: The Structure of British Television in the Nineties*, London: Lawrence and Wishart.

Hooks, B. (1992), *Black Looks*, London: Turnaround.

Husband, C. (1989) *Video and Ethnic Minority Communities in Britain: A Research Report,* London: Broadcasting Research Unit.

Husband, C. (ed.) (1994), *A Richer Vision*, London: John Libbey.

Husband, C., Chouhan, J. M. (1985) 'Local Radio in the Communication Environment of Ethnic Minorities in Britain' in T. Van Dijk (ed.), *Discourse and Communication.* Berlin: Walter de Gruyter, pp. 270-94.

Hussein, A. (1994) 'Market Forces and the Marginalization of Black Film and Video Production in the United Kingdom' in C. Husband (ed.) *A Richer Vision,* London: John Libbey, pp.127-42.

Independent Television Commission (ITC) (1993), *Annual Report and Accounts, 1993*, London: ITC.

Independent Television Commission (ITC) (1994) 'Ethnic Minorities', ITC Notes, No. 37, London: ITC.

Independent Television Commission (ITC) (1996), *Annual Report and Accounts, 1996*, London: ITC.

Ismond, P. (1994) *Ethnic Minority Media Production in Relation to*

British Media Policies, unpublished PhD Thesis, University of Bradford.

Jenkins, R. (1986), *Racism and Recruitment,* Cambridge: Cambridge University Press.

Jones, M. and Dungey, J. (1983) *Ethnic Minorities and Television,* Centre for Mass Communication Research, Leicester: University of Leicester.

Jones, T. (1993) *Britain's Ethnic Minorities,* London: Policy Studies.

Keighron, P. and Walker, C. (1994) 'Working in Television: Five Interviews' in S. Hood (ed.) *Behind the Screens: The Structure of British Television in the Nineties,* London: Lawrence and Wishart.

MacDonald, J.F. (1992) *Blacks and White TV,* Chicago: Nelson Hall.

Mercer, K. (ed.) (1988) *Black Film, Black Cinema,* ICA Documents 7: British Film Institute.

Mercer, K. (1989) 'General Introduction', in T. Daniels and J. Gerson (eds.) *The Colour Black: Black Images in British Television,* London: British Film Institute, pp.1-11.

Mercer, K. (1994) *Welcome to the Jungle,* London: Routledge.

Morar, N. (1995) 'Multicultural Programmes Department' Department Publication, BBC Pebble Mill, Birmingham.

Murdock, G. (1984) 'Reporting the Riots: Images and Impacts' in J.Benyon (ed.), *Scarman and After,* Oxford: Pergamon.

Murdock, G. (1994) 'Money Talks: Broadcasting, Finance and Public Culture' in S. Hood (ed.) *Behind the Screens: The Structure of British Television in the Nineties,* London: Lawrence and Wishart.

Murray, N. (1986) 'Anti-Racists and Other Demons: The Press and Ideology in Thatcher's Britain', *Race and Class,* XXVII : 1-20.

Negrine, R. (1990), 'British Television in an Age of Change', in K. Dyson and P. Humphreys (eds.) *The Political Economy of Communications,* London: Routledge, pp.148-170.

Neil, A. (ed.) (1982) *The Cable Revolution: Britain on the Brink of the Information Society,* Crawley: Visionhire Cable.

O'Huie, W. (1987) 'Cable Access and the Teaching of Video

Production, a Review and Assessment', *Journal of Film and Video*, 39(3): 40-55.

Parvin, S. (1989), *The Communication Environment of the Bangladeshi Community in Bradford*, unpublished PhD thesis, Bradford: University of Bradford.

Peach, C. (1996) 'A Question of Collar', *The Times Higher*, August 23rd, p.17.

Peak, S. (ed.) (1995) *The Media Guide*, London: Fourth Estate.

Peak, S. and Fisher, P. (eds.) (1996) *The Media Guide*, London: Fourth Estate.

Phillips, T. (1992) 'Trevor Phillips' Interview in J. Pines (ed.) *Black and White in Colour*, London: British Film Institute Publishing.

Phillips, T. (1995) 'UK TV: A Place in the Sun' in C. Frachon and M. Vargaftig (eds.), *European Television*, London: John Libbey.

Phillips, T. (1996) 'Are We Getting the Big Picture?' *The Guardian*, June 10, pp.12-13.

Phillips-Eteng, E. (1988), *Black British Consumer Markets*, London: The Planners Guide.

Pines, J. (1988) 'Black Independent Film in Britain: Historical Overview' in J. Twitchin (ed.), *The Black and White Media Show Book*, Stoke on Trent: Trentham Books, pp.103-111.

Pines, J. (ed.) (1992) *Black and White in Colour*, London: British Film Institute Publishing.

Robins, K. and Cornford, J. (1992) 'What is "Flexible" About Independent Producers?' *Screen*, 33(2): 190-200.

Ross, K. (1996) *Black and White Media*, Oxford: Polity Press.

Salam, S. (1995) 'A Mirror Crack'd From Side to Side: Black and Independent Producers and the Television Industry' in C. Frachon and M. Vargaftig (eds.), *European Television*, London: John Libbey.

Schudson, M. (1991) 'The Sociology of News Production Revisited' in J. Curran and M. Gurevitch (eds.), *Mass Media and Society*, London: Edward Arnold.

Shah, S. (1992) 'Samir Shah' Interview in J. Pines (ed.) *Black and White in Colour*, London: British Film Institute Publishing.

Smith, D.J. (1977), *Racial Disadvantage in Britain: The PEP Report*, Harmondsworth: Penguin.

Snead, J. (1994) 'Black Independent Film: Britain and America' in J. Snead, *White Screens: Black Images,* London: Routledge.

Solomos, J. and Black, L. (1996) *Racism and Society*, London: Macmillan.

Sparks, C. (1994) 'Independent Production: Unions and Casualization' in S. Hood (ed.) *Behind the Screens: The Structure of British Television in the Nineties*, London: Lawrence and Wishart.

Syedain, H. (1993) 'Major Minority Interest', *Marketing*, April 1, pp.37-40.

Tatla, D.S. and Singh, G. (1989) 'The Punjabi Press', *New Community*, 15(2): 171-84.

Taylor, J. (1994) 'The Professionals', *Sunday Times Magazine*, January 30, pp.4-5.

Troyna, B. (1981) *Public Awareness and the Media: A Study of Reporting on Race*, London: Commission for Racial Equality.

Tulloch, J. (1990) 'Television and Black Britons' in A. Goodwin and G. Whannel (eds.) *Understanding Television*, London: Routledge, pp. 141-52.

Tumber, H. (1982) *Television and the Riots.* Broadcasting Research Unit, London: British Film Institute.

Tunstall, J. (1993) *Television Producers*, London: Routledge.

Twitchin, J. (1988) 'Stereotypical Thinking in TV News and Current Affairs' in J. Twitchin (ed.), *The Black and White Media Show Book*, Stoke on Trent: Trentham Books, pp.214-35.

Van Dijk, T. (1991) *Racism and the Press*, London: Routledge.

Wadsworth, M. (1986) 'Racism in Broadcasting' in J. Curran (ed.) *Bending Reality - The State of the Media*, London: Pluto Press. pp.38-46.

Williams, G. (1994), *Media Ownership and Democracy*, London: Campaign for Press and Broadcasting Freedom.

Wilson. C.C. and Gutierrez, F. (1995) *Race, Multiculturalism, and the Media*, London: Sage.

Winston, B. (1994) 'Public Service in the New Broadcasting Age' in S. Hood (ed.), *Behind the Screens: The Structure of British Television in the Nineties*, London: Lawrence and Wishart.

Appendix

Semi-Structured Interview Schedules

Independents

General introduction to 'Ethnic Minorities and Television Research Programme', with reference to: aims, funding, dissemination of results, anonymity.

1)   Can you tell me briefly how you came to be involved in this area of work?

      a) Can you describe your current position/role(s)?

2)   Could you describe the general history of the company/organisation you are involved with and its general aims?

      Prompt re: sources of funding/sponsorship/resources/support/ production training/facilities/other

3)   Can you tell me about the sorts of minority ethnic programmes you have been involved with and/or hope to make in the future ('minority ethnic programmes' defined as 'made by', 'for' or 'about' ethnic minorities)?

4)   What general problems and difficulties have you and your organisation encountered concerning the production of minority ethnic programmes?

      a) Can you describe your dealings with other TV companies/institutions?

      b) Can you describe your dealings, if any, with Channel Four?

      c) How, if at all, have these changed through time?

5)   What are your organisations aims regarding minority ethnic programmes?

      a) What aims do you think organisation's like yours should have regarding minority ethnic programmes?

      b) What can/should organisations like yours contribute that 'mainstream' producers cannot?

      c) What responsibility or role do you think your organisation should have in relation to wider minority communities?

d) Do you feel an expectation from the minority communities to produce certain types of programmes?

6) What do you consider to be the most important issues confronting producers of minority ethnic TV programmes now, and in the future?

7) Other

BBC in-house producers

General introduction to 'Ethnic Minorities and Television Research Programme', with reference to: aims, funding, dissemination of results, anonymity.

1) Can you tell me briefly how you came to be involved in this area of work?

a) Can you describe your current position/role(s)?

2) Could you describe the general programme department policy/remit in relation to your programme making activity?

3) Can you tell me about the sorts of minority ethnic programmes you have been involved with and/or hope to make in the future ('minority ethnic programmes' defined as 'made by', 'for' or 'about' ethnic minorities)?

4) What general problems and difficulties have you and your department encountered concerning the production of minority ethnic programmes?

Prompt: pre-production, production, post-production

5) What, if any, contact do you have with other TV production companies and Channel Four?

How have these changed through time?

6) What aims do you think organisations like yours should have regarding minority ethnic programmes?

7) What can/should departments/organisations like yours contribute that independent producers cannot, and vice versa?

a) What responsibility or role do you think your organisation should have in relation to wider minority communities?

b) What contact do you have with wider ethnic minority communities?

d) Do you feel an expectation from the minority communities to produce certain types of programmes?

8)   What do you consider to be the most important issues confronting producers of minority ethnic TV programmes now, and in the future?

9)   Other

Author/Name Index

Ali, S. 207
Alibhai-Brown, Y. 184
Anwar, M. 20n
AsiaNet/AsiaVision 15, 17,
23n, 164, 166-193, 198, 201,
203, 205, 206, 207
Arts Council 137
Avon County Council 128

Back, L. 22n
Barry, A. 3
BBC 7, 8, 13, 15, 16, 17, 18,
25-96, 99, 100, 102, 104, 129,
130, 136, 137, 138, 139, 141,
142, 143, 151, 153, 155, 156,
157, 159, 163, 164, 167, 173,
184, 185, 201, 202, 211-218,
228-229
*BBC Multicultural Pro-
grammes Department (Asian
Programmes Department)* 15,
16, 17, 25-96, 142, 211-218
BFI (British Film Institute) 9,
127, 137
Bhatt, A. 21n, 120
Black Audio Film Collective 9
*Black Entertainment Television
(BET)* 161, 194, 195, 198,
200, 204
Black Pyramid 127
Bristol City Council 128
Broadcasting Act 1990 125,
137, 147, 214
Butterworth, E. 2
Bygrave, M. 180

CableTel 170
Central Television 21n, 143
Chan, J.M. 174
Channel Four 4, 7, 8, 16, 76,
77, 78, 127, 130, 131, 133-134,
136-139, 145-153, 156, 157,

Taylor, J. 200
Telecommunications Incorporated 194
Tracey, M. 147, 148
Troyna, B. 3
Tulloch, J. 4
Tumber, H. 3
Tunstall, J. 12
TV Asia 23n, 66, 161, 181, 189, 190
Twitchin, J. 3

Van Dijk, T. 3

Wadsworth, M. 4
Walker, C. 9
Williams, G. 174, 200
Wilson, C. C. 6
Winston, B. 7

Yorkshire TV 130

ZTV 66, 158, 162